Teaching Handbook

Y4/P5

Maureen Lewis
Series Editor

OXFORD

Project X Creative Team

Series Editor: Maureen Lewis

Series Consultants: Christine Cork (Primary Strategy Consultant, Kent) and Pippa Doran (Senior English Advisor, Kent)

Scottish Consultants: Louise Ballantyne (Project Manager Literacy, LTS) and Sue Ellis (University of Strathclyde)

Lead Author: (character books): Tony Bradman

Illustrator: (character books): Jon Stuart, Jonatronix Ltd

***Guided/Group Reading Notes* author team:** Maureen Lewis, Jo Tregenza, Amanda Snowden, Sue Huxley, Anne Derry, Katie Frost

Project X concept by Rod Theodorou and Emma Lynch

The publisher wishes to thank the following schools for their valuable contribution to the trialling and development of Project X:

Hawkedon Primary School, Reading; Bordesley Green Primary School, Birmingham; Witton Gilbert Primary School, Durham; St Patricks RC VA Primary School, Consett; St Andrew's CE Primary School, Rochdale; Temple Primary School, Manchester; West Denton First School, Newcastle Upon Tyne; Wardley Primary School, Gateshead; New Hinksey CE Primary School, Oxford; New Marston Primary School, Oxford; St Andrews CE Primary School, Oxford; Sunningwell CE Primary School, Abingdon; St Nicolas CE Primary School, Abingdon; Lee Mount Primary School, Halifax; Long Wittenham CE Primary School, Abingdon; Charlton On Otmoor Primary School, Oxford; Carnmoney Primary School, County Antrim; Stracathro Primary School, Angus; James Gillespie Primary School, Edinburgh; Malcolm Primary School, London; Sherborne CE Primary School, Cheltenham

OXFORD
UNIVERSITY PRESS

is a department of the University of Oxford.
It furthers the University's objective of excellence in research, scholarship, and education by publishing worldwide.

Text and illustrations © Oxford University Press 2009

Acknowledgements
The publisher would like to thank the following for permission to reproduce photographs:
p12t Tony Bradman; **p12**b Jon Stuart, **p14** OUP/photodisk; **p56** Monkey Business Images/Shutterstock; All other photography © OUP/ MTJ Media.

Photocopy master illustration by Michael Garton and character illustration by Jon Stuart

First published in 2009

Project X concept by Rod Theodorou and Emma Lynch

ISBN: 978-0-19-847012-0

1 3 5 7 9 10 8 6 4 2

Printed in Great Britain by Bell & Bain

Paper used in the production of this book is a natural, recyclable product made from wood grown in sustainable forests. The manufacturing process conforms to the environmental regulations of the country of origin.

Contents

Project X – Structure and components   4

Welcome to Project X   6

Project X – Turning boys into real readers   7

The Project X character books   10

Creating the Project X character books   12

Learning to read with Project X   14

The cluster structure of Project X   22

Using Project X for Guided reading   23

Reading behaviours checklist   25

Progression and planning   26

Primary Framework objectives   26

Project X and the *Curriculum for Excellence*   28

Project X and the National Curriculum in Wales   34

Project X and the Primary Curriculum for Northern Ireland   36

Assessing Pupils' Progress   38

Assessment record sheets   41
     Self assessment sheets   44
     Comprehension assessment chart   47
     Reading partners and celebrating achievement   48
     Reading and writing certificates   50

Running records   52
     Running record sheet   55

Reading at home – working with parents/carers   56

Project X – Using a thematic approach   58

Photocopy Masters   62

     PCMs 1-21 – follow up activities for each Project X book

     PCMs 22-35 – generic PCMs can be used with any book

Project X – Structure and components

Year Group	Book Band	ORT Stage	Cluster Packs – five books linked by a theme, plus guided/group reading notes									
Reception /P1	1	1+										
	2	2										
	3	3										
Year 1/P2	4	4										
	5	5										
	6	6										
Year 2/P3	7	7										
	8	8										
	9	9										
	10	10										
	11	11										
Year 3/P4	11	11										
	12	10 11										
Year 4/P5	13	12 13										

4

Teachers' Resources		Interactive Resources
Teaching Handbook		6 stories to read and explore
Teaching Handbook		6 stories to read and explore
Teaching Handbook	Project X Handbook: Raising Reading Achievement for Boys • Proven strategies for getting boys reading • Practical advice to help you make it happen Girls will benefit, too!	6 stories to read and explore
Teaching Handbook		6 stories to read and explore
Teaching Handbook		

Welcome to Project X!

Project X is a an innovative new reading programme designed to hook young children in to reading in Reception/P1, support them in their early reading development, and turn them into confident, independent and enthusiastic readers by the time they reach Year 4/P5.

The series of 140 stunning and highly original books offers an interesting, exciting and motivating choice of reading materials for 21st century children. These include top quality stories by some of the very best writers for children, fascinating information books, and electronic texts supported by audio and visual media. Whilst designed to appeal to all children, the books give special attention to the needs and tastes of boy readers – a benefit outlined in more detail on pages 7–9.

Motivation is crucial to the success of most readers, particularly boys. For this reason, the teaching and learning approaches underpinning **Project X** emphasize the importance of comprehension and engagement in learning to read. The books have been developed, first and foremost, to be *great reads*, although the importance of developing decoding and word recognition skills in the early stages of reading is not overlooked. The action-packed stories and fascinating non-fiction material provide ample opportunities for children to apply and reinforce their decoding skills, in line with the pace and progression in phonics recommended by *Letters and Sounds*.

What makes Project X different?

- **Project X** is a new generation guided reading programme especially designed to appeal to boys and to help raise reading standards for all your pupils.
- It is **truly boy-friendly** in its content, design, structure, and teaching and learning approach.
- It contains an **amazing new character adventure** that will hook children in to reading and keep them reading.
- It offers **unique thematic clusters** of books on topics that children will love – great for motivation, supporting progress and linking to the wider curriculum.
- It offers **exceptional support for guided reading**, with easy to use notes and advice on assessment for learning.
- It is the **perfect complement to your existing resources** – Book Banded and linked to Oxford Reading Tree stages.

Project X – Turning boys into real readers

Project X has been created to meet the needs and interests of all children. However, there is a wealth of research showing that there are specific challenges involved in ensuring some boys become and remain readers. Boys are more likely than girls to struggle with reading and to give up on independent reading. Boys are also far more likely than girls to under perform in writing. In the *Rose Review* of March 2006, Jim Rose identified: "urgent concerns about the generally weaker performance of boys than girls".

For these reasons **Project X** has been designed to include content and elements of teaching and learning practice which will particularly support boys while not disadvantaging girls.

Research also shows that in schools where there is little or no achievement gap between girls and boys, teachers:

- have high expectations of all the children in the class
- avoid gender or other stereotyping
- use an active teaching style
- try to get all children involved
- make use of formative assessment.

Project X supports teachers in embedding such approaches into their practice.

Why do boys struggle with reading?

The reasons for some boys' underperformance in literacy are complex and often include wider societal factors such as gender roles and stereotypes, family influences, behaviour issues, peer pressure and self-stereotyping. There are also factors relating directly to the teaching of reading such as boys' early reading experiences, teacher expectations, teaching and learning *practise*s, learning contexts and book choice. One factor, however, stands out above all others when it comes to boys and learning and that is *motivation*. When it comes to reading and writing boys, far more than girls, need to see a clear purpose for what they are doing. They won't simply do something because they are told to; they want to know what's in it for them. For some boys it is not that they can't, it is just that they can't be bothered!

As well as motivating content, a number of teaching and learning *practise*s have been shown to be successful in addressing gender issues in school and in supporting boy readers. All of these have been incorporated into **Project X**.

Book choice and content

The **Project X** books reflect the genres that we know boys love, whilst offering a good range of materials to broaden their reading experiences. The stories, written mostly by male authors, are fast-paced and full of action, adventure, humour and fantasy and the emphasis on character is guaranteed to hook readers in. The design of some of the books includes those 'comic book' conventions, such as visual literacy, so popular with boys. The non-fiction book topics have been chosen specifically to appeal to boy readers and to be both interesting and challenging.

Social identity

Readers can confirm and extend their own identity through reading and so build their confidence and engagement. The core characters in **Project X** think, act and feel in ways that modern children, particularly boys, will be able to relate to. However they do not represent gender stereotypes. They show both active and affective aspects of identity. The non-fiction books present inspirational role models such as high achieving sports personalities, and include content that emphasizes teamwork, dealing with difficult emotions, individual endeavour and people facing the challenges of everyday life.

The importance of talk

Discussing and reflecting on books is a vital part of becoming an engaged reader and talking to gather ideas is an important strategy for becoming a writer. Boys in particular benefit from articulating and reinforcing their thoughts and ideas through talk. The **Project X** books have been developed to offer a wealth of discussion opportunities, and speaking and listening strategies and activities are embedded throughout the teaching support.

Experiential, creative and reflective follow-up activities

Boys – and in fact most learners – tend to prefer active and experiential ways of learning to sitting still and being silent! The teaching ideas provided with each **Project X** book include suggestions for physical experiences to support active learning. The wide range of literacy and cross-curricular follow-up activities include many ideas for interactive teaching and learning and address a range of teaching and learning styles – aural, visual, kinaesthetic.

Regular reviews of progress and target setting

Boys like to have clear learning targets in order to understand their reason for learning. They also like to see evidence of their progress as they find achievement and recognition motivating. Each guided/group reading session provided in the **Project X** *Guided/Group Reading Notes* has a clear focus – with targets and assessment criteria that can be used for regular learning reviews. There are also peer and self assessment sheets for children to record their progress (see pages 44-46).

ICT and multimedia literacy

Today's children are growing up in a multimedia world. As well as being highly engaging and motivating for children, films, cartoons, websites, computer games and other multimedia texts often present specific and sophisticated literacy challenges. It is important that pupils' experience in using such forms of literacy is acknowledged, appreciated and developed if they are to be fully literate in the 21st century.

Project X responds to this in two ways. Firstly, the series aims to engage young readers by using a detailed, 3D digital illustration style for the character books. This brings the world of films and computer games to books and has been a huge hit with children in our trials. Secondly, **Project X** offers a collection of stories on screen that include audio, animation and video elements to engage children, stimulate discussion and support both traditional and multimedia literacy skills.

Family involvement

Building a reading culture at home as well as in school is important so that boys see reading as something to engage with beyond the school environment. Involving fathers or other males in reading with boys has been shown to be successful in encouraging this. Some specific advice on involving parents in their children's reading is given in this Handbook (see pages 56–57) and each of the **Project X** books contains some simple questions and activities to support parents/carers in reading with their children.

Reading role models

It is important for boys to see others, particularly other males, reading. This reinforces the place that reading has in society. Many of the **Project X** stories have purposeful uses of literacy woven in to the plot and the core characters – Max, Cat, Ant and Tiger – are often shown reading and writing for different purposes.

Competitive approaches

Much of the research into raising boys' achievement shows that competitive approaches to learning can be effective. This doesn't mean setting children against each other but against their own personal targets. On pages 44-46 you will find self-assesment sheets for each level of the **Project X** books in Year 4/P5 and these can be used to help children track their own progress against their reading targets.

Celebration of achievement

Ongoing praise, together with recognition and reward for success are vitally important to young learners, particularly boys. On pages 50–51 of this Handbook you will find reading and writing certificates templates that can be used to celebrate achievement.

What about the girls?

It is important to state that **Project X** is not just about boys. Girls too benefit from the kinds of teaching and learning outlined above. Additionally, almost all of the evidence from research, case studies and various Raising Boys' Achievement initiatives that fed in to the development of **Project X** shows that if you can engage boys with reading there are huge benefits for girls. Classroom reality often means that disengaged boys take up disproportionately more teacher time and that quiet, well-behaved, often middle ability girls suffer as a result. Engaged boys give teachers more time to ensure that every child is being helped to progress at the right pace. Girls can also benefit from the lively and imaginative discussion that engaged boys participate in – improving their comprehension skills and the quality of their writing.

In terms of content and book choice, girls are generally open to exploring a wide range of texts whilst boys are much more likely to have a narrower range of preferences. So whilst the **Project X** books have been developed to appeal to boys there is no reason why girls won't love them too! The character strand of **Project X** includes a strong girl character in Cat, an adult female heroine in the shape of Dani Day, and explores themes such as family and friendship that are traditionally seen to be appealing to girls.

> The *Raising the Reading Achievement of Boys* book that accompanies **Project X** gives more detailed information, advice and ideas for raising reading standards across your school.
> *Visit our website for details: www.OxfordPrimary.co.uk/projectx*

The Project X character books

Today's young children love **characters**. Almost all children's popular culture – from books to toys to TV to computer games – revolves around distinctive characters. Some are enduring favourites, like Spiderman, Scooby Doo, Postman Pat and Thomas the Tank Engine, but there are new characters being created all the time – Peppa Pig, Ben 10, Power Rangers ... the list is endless.

Following the adventures of well-loved characters is widely acknowledged as one of the best ways to hook young children in to reading ... and to keep them reading. At the heart of **Project X** lies a group of exciting new characters.

Meet the characters

Max

Project X follows the adventures of Max, Cat, Ant and Tiger – four children who one day discover four amazing watches that allow them to shrink. They have many fantastic and action-packed micro-adventures, exploring an ordinary world made extraordinary by their micro-size. It is a world in which they have power and independence, solve their own problems and gradually form strong, though often tested, bonds of friendship. The four children (three boys, one girl) have personalities and habits that today's children will be able to relate to, whilst providing positive role models for readers.

As the series progresses, the adventures evolve into episodes within an overarching 'soap' style story. The books can be read in any order and not all books have to be read, but in the background an exciting master plot is developing that readers from Year 2/P3 upwards will gradually uncover.

Cat

Within each thematic cluster of books in the series, there is also a non-fiction book featuring one or more of the characters as 'guides' who pose questions, reflect thoughts and make comment on the content. The use of character in a non-fiction context helps to engage the reader with the content and makes the books more interactive.

The character story in Year 4/P5

In Reception/P1 and Year 1/P2, the character story books feature a series of micro-adventures in familiar settings such as home, garden, park and school. Each book stands alone as a simple – yet amazing – micro-adventure. The four characters, their watches and their shrinking powers are introduced and developed so that the formula of the character strand becomes familiar.

Ant

In Year 2/P3 readers discover more about the origins of the four watches. There are hints of a mysterious creator and little spy robots begin to appear. The micro-adventures become more sophisticated and take our characters beyond the familiar locations and situations of the early levels.

In Year 3/P4 – or from Lime Band upwards – readers discover the truth about the watches and where they came from. They find out about the arch villain who created the watches – Dr X – and do battle with his X-bots. They also meet Dr X's comic henchmen, Plug and Socket, and team up with the heroic scientist Dani Day.

In Year 4/P5 – or at Grey Band – the amazing micro-adventures of Max, Cat, Ant and Tiger build towards a climax. All appears lost as the X-bots finally capture the children and Dr X retrieves his watches. Now he can activate his X machine and carry out his plans to shrink the world. Using all their

Tiger

ingenuity and courage the children and Dani Day manage to defeat Dr X and the villain is taken away by the police. The children are heroes and are invited to be interviewed by the world famous WOW! Magazine. At this point they discover two things: 1. the watches have developed a time travel function; 2. Dr X has escaped ...

All of the **Project X** books are designed to stand alone as complete adventures and it is not expected that every child will read every book. However, at Grey Band there are certain 'key' books which are best read in sequence in order to enhance children's understanding and enjoyment of the overarching plot.

Making a Stand – by Tony Bradman
(Dilemmas and decisions cluster)

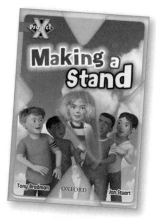

From her secret micro-hideout inside NASTI, Dani Day watches in horror as an army of X3 robots takes off in the new X-Craft to capture the children and their watches. She sends a warning message to Max but is then captured and her watch taken by a triumphant Dr X. At the last moment Dani escapes ...

Meanwhile, Plug and Socket are having second thoughts about working for Dr X but they too are captured in their feeble attempt to rebel. The children receive Dani's message. Now all they can do is wait ...

Revenge of the X-bots - by Anthony McGowan
(Great escapes cluster)

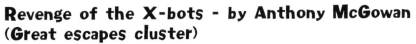

Max, Cat, Ant and Tiger spend the night camping in Ant's garden, on the look out for a comet. Instead of a comet they see a NASTI spacecraft, which beams them aboard. At first they fight off the X-bots and take control of the X-craft, but the X-bots regroup and overpower the children. To the children's horror the X-craft descends into NASTI headquarters, where Dr X is waiting for them ...

The X-machine – by Tony Bradman
(Great escapes cluster)

Dr X triumphantly takes the watches back from the children and sends them to join Plug and Socket in the NASTI cells. He slots the watches in to his X-machine and powers it up ... the world is about to be shrunk to micro-size! Then Dani Day appears to rescue the children and together they defeat Dr X, who is eventually zapped by his own machine and turned to micro-size. He is handed, quite literally, over to the police.

The WOW! Award – by Chris Powling
(In the news cluster)

Our four heroes – Max, Cat, Ant and Tiger – are on their way to be interviewed by the world's most famous magazine, WOW! In the limousine, Ant discovers a new power on his watch, but the others are so excited they pay him no attention. When they get to WOW! the children are even more excited to meet famous author K J Sparking, who has come to receive an award. In fact, they meet two K J Sparklings and must use their new time travel powers to discover the true identity of the fake K J Sparking ... none other than Dr X's mum, Mrs X!

To be continued ...

Creating the Project X character books

Max, Cat, Ant and Tiger are recognizable 21st century children and they are created on the page using modern, 3D computer-generated graphics. This gives them 'eye appeal' to children used to such sophisticated artwork from their very earliest years. This up-to-the minute design is coupled with texts written by the some of the very best children's authors.

The author team

The characters and the overarching story were created with the help of Tony Bradman – an experienced writer and editor of stories for children of all ages, best known for his *Dilly the Dinosaur* series. Through his writing and his many school visits and workshops, Tony brings to the series a passion for character and story and a genuine understanding of young readers' needs.

A core team of top quality writers – including Chris Powling, Anthony McGowan, Jan Burchett, Sara Vogler and Shoo Rayner – have worked alongside Tony on the character stories. Their challenge has been to maintain the continuity of character and plot whilst injecting a range of story ideas and writing styles to the series.

The illustrator

The stunning 3D illustrations created for **Project X** are the work of talented artist Jon Stuart and his team at Jonatronix Ltd. The artwork has involved the creation of thousands of character poses, props, settings and other amazing objects.

Each of the core characters is developed on a wire frame, allowing them to be moved, posed and positioned in the illustrations. Each character's face is made up of hundreds of 'virtual muscles', enabling us to create a range of detailed and authentic expressions.

Our illustrator works on a virtual film set, manipulating the characters and props and using a variety of textures and lighting techniques to create the stunning images you will see in the character books.

Project X brings the world of 3D animation and computer graphics to a reading programme for the very first time and is guaranteed to appeal to today's children!

More information about our authors and illustrator can be found at www.OxfordPrimary.co.uk/projectx

Learning to read with Project X

Teachers want all their pupils to learn to read. They also want them to become effective and enthusiastic readers who understand what they read and recognize both the pleasure and usefulness of reading. The **Project X** programme shares these aims. Research shows there are several important factors in helping children become successful readers who understand what they read and who enjoy reading. **Project X** draws on this research which emphasizes the importance of the following factors:

Speaking and listening

Children's oral language and their ability to listen to others are crucial to the development of thinking and communication skills and underpin much of their learning, including learning to read.

Children first develop their understanding about the sounds, rhythms and structures of words and texts through listening to and by creating their own spoken texts. Listening to texts being read aloud or engaging in dialogue about texts helps build a varied oral vocabulary which in turn impacts on learning to read.

Children can also extend their engagement with texts by discussing them and elaborating on them through drama and role play. Talking about texts and orally questioning texts supports the development of comprehension – and with understanding comes the motivation to read more. Talk also helps children to gather ideas for writing.

Supporting children to develop and extend the vital skills of speaking and listening is embedded in **Project X** through a range of imaginative suggestions for purposeful and contextualized speaking and listening, group interaction and drama activities.

Project X recognizes that children come to school with a range of language skills and life experiences. Children for whom English is an additional language, for example, may be fluent in their first language but at an early stage in the development of their English. The **Project X** books and software provide content to prompt discussion that will broaden children's contextual and linguistic knowledge and in turn support their understanding of a text. For example, many of the **Project X** stories open with an information page, designed to set the context for the story. They may end with a story map to stimulate recall and retelling. The thematic 'cluster' structure of the programme broadens children's knowledge and understanding and offers lots of opportunities for discussion and comparison.

Reading strategies

Decoding/encoding and word recognition

Project X is not primarily a phonics programme but it does recognize and support the role of phonics and decoding skills in the early stages of learning to read. By Year 4/P5 the majority of children will rarely use phonics to decode as they read. Most words will be recognized on sight and children's reading fluency will continue to increase the more they read. Occasionally they may still call on their phonic knowledge when they encounter a new word, splitting multisyllabic words into syllables or words within words to decode the sections they don't recognize. Phonic knowledge remains helpful for encoding in spelling and suggestions for spelling patterns to be found in the books are given in the *Guided/Group Reading Notes.*

The cluster structure of the books provides opportunities for revisiting and reinforcing vocabulary, particularly new or more challenging context words. Building vocabulary knowledge remains important for increasing reading fluency and comprehension so new vocabulary is often repeated within a text and across texts.

Context and syntactic clues

Fluent readers use a range of strategies when approaching an unknown word, and when monitoring for and building meaning. These cues continue to be important as the need for frequent decoding diminishes.

In using syntactic cues children use their implicit grammatical knowledge to identify the kind of word likely to be in the sentence (and to reject the kind of word unlikely to be there). The missing word in 'The cat ___ on the mat' is likely to be a verb such as lay, sat, slept and so on. It is unlikely to be words such as, blue (adjective) or under (preposition).

In using context cues children draw on their understanding of the meaning so far and their knowledge beyond the text to identify likely and unlikely words. 'The girl splashed in the pu ___' is more likely to be puddle than pudding, for example. Readers will also use the supporting images to help them work out new words or to clarify their understanding.

Using these cues is not encouraging children to 'guess' words. Rather, they encourage children to use logic, prior knowledge and linguistic knowledge to help them narrow the range of possibilities, and then use comprehension to check whether the word makes sense in the text.

Fluent readers will also reread sentences and passages to clarify meaning. They will tolerate a degree of ambiguity in a text where they recognize that they might not yet have all the information they need to fully understand the text – at the beginning of a long story for example as they encounter new characters and settings. In this case they will read on to seek clarification. In deciding whether clarification is needed or ambiguity can be tolerated, readers are building the metacognitive skills of monitoring and acting upon their own level of reading comprehension.

Teachers can demonstrate how and when to use these approaches during shared reading by explicitly discussing the decisions they are making, as a fluent reader, to monitor and enhance their reading comprehension. They should encourage children to reflect on how they are reading and understanding as well as what they are reading and understanding. Children can then be encouraged to do this themselves during guided and independent reading.

Comprehension

Building children's comprehension skills is given a high priority in **Project X**. Understanding what has been read is central to being an effective reader. Through making meaning within a text children become actively engaged with the text and can relate the text to their own world and life experiences, or extend these. If a child does not understand what they have read – even if they can recognize the words – they are unlikely to enjoy reading it.

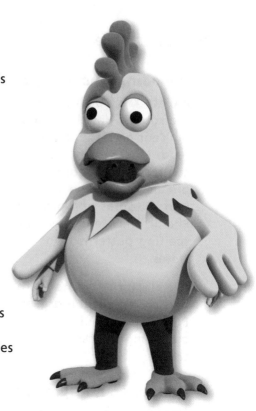

Comprehension is not something that comes automatically. The latest research shows that children can be helped to develop comprehension skills by the explicit teaching of certain aspects of comprehension and by offering children specific strategies to help build these aspects. **Project X** helps teachers to recognize the opportunities within each book to focus on specific aspects of comprehension. Learning strategies to support these aspects of comprehension are given. Over time children develop a repertoire of comprehension strategies that they can use across a range of texts.

Aspect of comprehension	Examples of some strategies
Previewing/predicting	Picture walk Prediction grid Freeze frame 'what if?' moments
Activating and building prior knowledge	KWLT sheet True/false/don't know reflection quiz
Questioning (teacher to child, child to child and child to text)	Online character/topic forums Role play Sticky note flurry Questions to a character/author
Recall	Story boards Picture prompts Retell to a talk partner
Visualization and other sensory responses	Visual story maps Creating small world scenes/animations Sensory prompt sheet
Deducing, inferring and drawing conclusions	Compare and contrast activities Inference grid
Synthesizing	1+1=2 grid
Summarizing/determining importance	Main ideas wheel 50 words or less challenges Structured overviews
Empathizing	Relationship charts Character 'self portraits' 'I say, do, think and feel' charts
Personal responses including adopting a critical stance	Response book diaries Alternative ending activities 'What if the opposite were true?' debates Decision Alley

Reading fluency

Understanding the importance of building reading fluency and having explicit strategies to achieve this are relatively neglected aspects of learning to read. Fluency occurs as children begin to recognize more and more words automatically and are not slowed down by the need to decode words individually. This recognition includes words that have initially been worked out phonetically and high and medium frequency words that are not phonetically regular. Contextualized repetition of words throughout a text and across texts, and frequent opportunities to reread texts, are important strategies for developing the fluency that comes with automatic word recognition. Word games and vocabulary building activities also play their part.

Further aspects of reading fluency are increasing the pace of reading from a slow word by word articulation, and the development of prosody – the rhythms and stresses used when reading (or talking) that help emphasize meaning. Some competent readers remain slow readers (in the sense of reading pace) or inexpressive readers. Initially, children might be expected to read fluently on texts which are familiar. This is one reason why opportunities to reread texts are important. As their reading ability progresses this behaviour should begin to appear on unfamiliar texts.

The Grey band books contain more complex language structures including both compound and complex sentences. Language play (puns, homophones, homonyms, codes, jokes, onomatopoeic words and so on) can be found in the texts. Expressive, descriptive and figurative language and vocabulary help create moods and emotions. Plots are more complex. This complexity of structure, language and syntax offers opportunities to discuss the author's craft and the impact of particular language choices. Understanding decisions such as starting a sentence with 'Suddenly,' or the impact of embedding a phrase within a complex sentence helps children build expression and fluency into their reading and provides models for their writing.

The support materials for **Project X** draw on the latest research into developing fluency. Listening to books being read aloud is one of the most effective ways to support the development of fluency – as well as a love of books – in developing readers. As teachers read aloud they model expressive, fluent reading. Unfortunately, regularly reading aloud to the class may be something teachers struggle to find time for beyond the early years. It may also be absent at home. The **Project X** software offers audio visual versions of some of the character stories to provide models of fluent, expressive reading. The *Guided/Group Reading Notes* include ideas for developing pace and prosody through purposeful 'read aloud' activities, drama and role play. Children might also enjoy recording themselves reading the texts or reading them aloud to a reading partner or younger children.

Building vocabulary

Beyond a certain range of everyday vocabulary, most new vocabulary is encountered through reading. However, if any individual word is not understood – even if it can be decoded – it can cause problems with understanding of the sentence or passage or text. There is a vicious circle in which poor readers (often those with poor oral language as well) have a limited vocabulary and therefore encounter more words they don't understand in a text. This makes reading harder for these children and often puts them off reading when reading is the key to a wider vocabulary. Explicit work on enriching children's vocabulary – equipping them with a large bank of words they understand – is therefore vital to building fluency, comprehension and motivation.

Research recommends:

- teaching both specific words and word-learning strategies
- seeing and meeting new vocabulary in rich contexts provided by authentic texts
- using 'rich' vocabulary instruction i.e. going beyond just defining a word to get children actively engaged in using new words and thinking about word meanings
- fostering word consciousness by encouraging an awareness of and interest in words
- ensuring multiple exposures to words in multiple contexts.

The books and support materials for **Project X** incorporate all of these approaches and the cluster structure of the programme is ideal for reinforcing new vocabulary in a range of different contexts.

The interdependence of reading and writing

Reading and writing are mutually supportive skills – which is why those children who don't understand what it is to be a reader usually struggle to become writers. By helping to engage children in reading, **Project X** also aims to support and inspire children's writing.

Throughout the *Guided/Group Reading Notes* there are many opportunities to examine the writer's craft and voice, explore the use of literary and informational language and the use of varied vocabulary and sentence structures. The structure of a variety of genres can also be explored. After each book there are several fun and contextualized activities designed to develop children's writing skills – with both short and long writing tasks suggested. There is always a clear purpose for the writing task, and talk, role play and drama activities are included as a means to stimulate ideas. Oral composition and rehearsal with a talk partner are also encouraged.

The **Project X** books offer models for children's own writing and the themes and character books in particular provide plenty of inspiration.

Character assets and 'clip art' to support children's writing about the **Project X** characters can be found on the accompanying software. The stories on the software can also be explored with a whole class or groups of children and the writer's craft examined through editing and annotation of the text.

Themes and cross-curricular learning

One way of supporting children's learning is to help them see how different aspects of their learning link together. This gives breadth and depth to learning and enables children to see the relevance of what they are learning to their own lives, to other aspects of school learning and learning beyond school. Research indicates that boys in particular favour approaches to learning that help them recognize its relevence to their lives and make links. A cross-curricular approach to learning can help them to do this.

Project X has been designed around a cluster structure in which five books are linked by a theme. The themes have been chosen to be interesting and child-friendly, often reflecting their interests beyond school rather than strictly 'curricula' based themes. Nevertheless, links to the other subjects within the National Curriculum can be made, as can links to wider skills such as thinking, creativity and problem solving.

The *Guided/Group Reading Notes* for each cluster highlight the cross-curricular opportunities offered by each theme, and there are further ideas for developing a thematic approach on pages 58–61 of this Handbook.

The importance of motivation

Learning to read and continuing reading to become an engaged and enthusiastic reader can be difficult – as with all learning, some children will struggle more than others. But if children want to read, and see reading as a valuable and enjoyable activity, they are far more likely to be motivated to 'stick at it'. Research shows that being well motivated impacts on learning outcomes.

Project X aims to support motivation by offering high quality books that children will enjoy reading. The character books within the series (see pages 10–13) play a key part in this. Firstly, the development of a set of main characters provides role models children can identify with and will want to read about. Secondly, the character books include an intriguing 'soap' style plot that develops over several levels and is designed to motivate children to want to read on – to find out what happens. The non-fiction books also aim to intrigue and engage readers.

For some children, however, such motivational content is not enough on its own and external motivational strategies can help. Boys in particular respond well to praise and to motivational rewards. The **Project X** self assessment sheets (see pages 44–46) where children record their reading progress and **Project X** certificates (see pages 50-51) can all be used to boost motivation as well as record progress.

Creativity and thinking skills

There is worldwide recognition of the need for 21st century learners to develop the skills of 'learning to learn' rather than continuing to focus solely on subject knowledge. The follow-up activities suggested in the **Project X** *Guided/Group Reading Notes* for each book offer many opportunities to develop creative thinking and skills such as reasoning, evaluation and problem solving. The underpinning cross-curricular skill of communication is supported through the many suggestions for speaking and listening, drama and writing as well as suggestions for communicating through music and dance.

The overall structure of **Project X** – with the character story developing across clusters and throughout the levels – encourages creative thinking by offering possibilities for children to 'generate and extend ideas, suggest hypotheses, apply imagination, and look for alternative innovative outcomes'. (QCA definition of creative thinking)

The role of multimedia in children's lives and learning

Children are involved with IT and multimedia, multimodal texts well before they start school. Picture books, television, computer games and the Internet are so commonplace in modern homes that it is important to recognize and acknowledge these reading experiences and the specific literacy skills they require.

The 3D look and feel of the **Project X** character books is designed to bring the appeal of cartoons and computer games to reading – inspiring the 'Playstation Generation' to see books as a valid part of their learning and entertainment culture.

The **Project X** software provides a selection of the character stories as interactive electronic texts for use on a computer or interactive whiteboard. These texts include audio and animation that will really bring the stories to life for today's developing readers. Each story can be read through or listened to and then explored and annotated using the tools provided. To accompany each story is a collection of multimedia assets – video clips, audio, animation and images – to inspire talk and to help set the context for the story before reading. The software also contains a selection of writing frames and 3D images from the character books for children to use in their own writing – either in print or on screen.

Creating a positive reading environment

An engaging and purposeful literacy environment is an important element of effective classrooms. It creates interest in reading and writing and offers many different opportunities for reading, writing, speaking and listening (including ICT based opportunities). It offers good models, learning prompts and resources to support learners in developing their literacy skills.

Such an environment includes an attractive book area with support materials and play/ drama opportunities to encourage children to make links between their reading and wider learning. Role play areas are often abandoned as children move from the lower to upper primary year groups. Those primary classrooms that retain elements of role play practice, perhaps in the form of a themed area, report that these continue to stimulate creative responses, talk, drama and prompts into writing.

The cross-curricular charts for each cluster (see pages 59–61) give specific suggestions for the learning environment including a role play area that will encourage creative play and purposeful uses of literacy.

A wide range of texts

- Attractive, age-appropriate books, both fiction and non-fiction
- Collections of books linked to the theme/s being studied in class
- Other reading materials including comics, graphic novels, brochures, catalogues, magazines, manuals and so on
- Children's own published writing
- Audio and/or visual texts such as talking stories, films and videos
- Dictionaries, atlases and children's thesaurus

Role play or themed area

- Related to a theme, a book, or an environment
- Labels, signs and other appropriate environmental text
- Small world play figures, toys, construction equipment, puppets and other materials to encourage the enactment, extension and creation of stories and information
- Materials for writing

A good literacy environment includes:

Displays

- Posters, charts and so on related to particular books, characters and authors
- Learning prompts such as an alphabet frieze, word lists, learning strategy posters, writing frameworks and so on
- Children's book reviews and other purposeful writing
- Labels, signs and notices for children to read in context

Vocabulary resources

- Word walls, word lists, word webs, word family charts
- Photographs and other images related to new vocabulary
- Word games - Scrabble, word snap. etc.
- Word of the Week and topic word displays

A comfy space

- Carpet, mats or cushions to make the reading area comfortable and inviting

The cluster structure of Project X

At all levels of **Project X**, the books are arranged in 'clusters' of five books that are linked by a theme. At Year 4/P5 there are three clusters (fifteen books) at Grey Band.

Each cluster contains:

- 2 character stories
- 1 character non-fiction book
- 1 variety story (not including the core characters)
- 1 variety non-fiction book (not including the core characters)

> These five books make up the Dilemmas and Decisions cluster at Grey Band.

All the books in a cluster are at the same reading level, although each book offers different aspects of support and challenge for the reader. The three clusters provide ample consolidation as children become increasingly independent readers. Building confidence and fluency at a level helps readers become secure in their view of themselves as readers.

The benefits of this cluster approach are:

- the themes are designed to be interesting and motivating for young readers, particularly boys
- the mix of fiction and non-fiction books offers different ways in to a theme for different reading tastes – yet helps to encourage the reader's interest across a range of books
- the themes enable children to meet key new words many times in different contexts, thus building their range of and confidence with new vocabulary
- as the reader progresses through the books on a theme (in any sequence) their familiarity with the context and vocabulary grows – this increases their confidence as readers, improves their word recognition, comprehension and fluency skills, and ensures that every reader makes progress
- the themes offer rich contexts for talk, drama and writing
- the themes provide many meaningful links between literacy and the wider curriculum.

The cluster themes provided at Year 4/P5 are as follows:

Book Band	Oxford Reading Tree Stage	Project X Themes
13 – Grey	Stages 12-13	Dilemmas and Decisions Great Escapes In the News

Using Project X for Guided reading

The **Project X** books have been written and levelled to help you deliver effective guided reading sessions, although they can also be used for independent reading.

Some children may progress more quickly through a level whilst others may need to spend more time at a level before moving on. It is important to undertake regular assessments of your guided reading groups to ensure that individual children are correctly supported and challenged.

Project X levels and progression in reading

Year Group					Book Band	National Curriculum Level
R/ P1	Y1/ P2	Y2/ P3	Y3/ P4	Y4/ P5		
					Band 1 Pink	Working towards Level 1 (RA approx below 5 yrs)
					Band 2 Red	Working towards Level 1 (RA approx below 5 yrs)
					Band 3 Yellow	Working just within Level 1 (RA approx just 5 yrs)
					Band 4 Blue	Working within Level 1 (RA approx 5 yrs +)
					Band 5 Green	Working within Level 1 (RA approx 5.5 yrs)
					Band 6 Orange	Working towards Level 2 (RA approx 6 yrs)
					Band 7 Turquoise	Working towards Level 2 (RA approx 6.5 yrs)
					Band 8 Purple	Working just within Level 2 (RA approx 7yrs)
					Band 9 Gold	Working within Level 2 (RA approx 7.5 yrs)
					Band 10 White	Working towards Level 3 (RA approx 8 yrs)
					Band 11 Lime	Working towards and just within Level 3 (RA approx 8.5 yrs)
					Band 12 Brown	Working within Level 3 (RA approx 9 -9.5 yrs)
					Band 13 Grey	Working towards Level 4 (RA approx 10 yrs +)

■ Expected Book Band range for majority of children in this year group

■ Normal Band range for tracking back for less able readers in this year group

□ Normal Band range for tracking forward for more able readers in this year group

The books in each cluster can be used flexibly, depending on the needs and tastes of the guided reading group. You may want to encourage the group to select a book from the theme for each session. Or you may want to choose some books from the cluster for use in guided reading and use others for independent or paired reading.

With the longer texts at Grey Band a book may be read over two or three guided reading sessions. Or only part of the book – a section or chapter – will be read in the guided reading session, preceded and/or followed by the rest of the book being read independently.

There are *Guided/Group Reading Notes* to support every book, with enough sessions to cover each book completely through guided reading if you wish to do so. There are also a wide range of ideas for follow-up work. How you manage this material, and how much of it you use, will depend on your overall needs and planning and the rate at which children's reading ability progresses.

Grouping children for guided reading

For guided reading sessions children are placed in groups of approximately six children of similar reading ability. Books are selected at the appropriate instructional level for each group – for guided reading, this means that children should be able to read the text with 90% accuracy. The Reading Behaviour checklist (see page 25) and/or the Running Record assessment sheet (see page 55) can be used to help you establish and regularly assess the appropriate guided reading level for an individual child or group.

Once the correct instructional level is established most children will then progress through the **Project X** books, which have been carefully levelled to Book Bands to ensure a gradual increase in reading challenge. The books for each level contain many familiar words likely to be recognized automatically, plus an appropriate degree of challenge around which the guided teaching and learning will focus.

The *Guided/Group Reading Notes* provide support for the following teaching sequence for every book in a cluster:

* before reading
* during reading
* after reading
* follow-up work – including talk, drama, writing, ICT and cross-curricular activities.

For each book, there are clear learning objectives, targets and prompts for ongoing assessment linked to the QCA Reading Assessment focuses – an overview of objectives and assessment focuses is given on pages 38–39 of this Handbook.

Independent reading

Children should be offered plenty of opportunities for wider independent reading of texts at a variety of levels. Rereading familiar or favourite texts, even those considered 'easy', as well as tackling 'hard' but highly engaging texts, are necessary experiences for building confidence, fluency and a love of reading.

The **Project X** books are ideal for independent reading. But you will also want to make available a range of books from other programmes, favourite texts, picture books, information books, comic books, magazines, etc. for children to select from. Opportunities for children to make their own choice of books for independent reading is important in allowing them to develop the personal preferences essential to reading engagement.

Reading Behaviours Checklist

This checklist – supported by your own knowledge of each child – can be used at any time to assess children's reading behaviours in order to determine or review their guided reading level. Not all children in Year 4/P5 will be reading at Grey band, so behaviours are given to enable you to track back to earlier bands if required.

A child that is mostly **low** in the behaviours at a given band needs to be reading at a lower band.
A child that is mostly **secure** in the behaviours at a given band is at the right reading level.
A child that is mostly **high** in the behaviours at a given band needs to be reading at a higher band.

Name of child:

Date:

Book Band	NC Level	Reading Behaviours	Low	Secure	High
White/ Lime	Towards Level 3	Can read silently most of the time			
		Can automatically relate unknown words to known words			
		Can sustain interest in a longer text and return to it confidently after a break			
		Can search for and find information in a text			
		Shows increased awareness of wide range of vocabulary and precise meanings			
		Can give and discuss opinions about a text			
Brown (Year 3/P4)	Within Level 3	Can sustain silent reading to include longer, more complex texts			
		Can read aloud with intonation and expression – particularly dialogue			
		Can recognize an increasing range of words automatically			
		Can identify ideas and themes within a text, making clear references			
		Can search for, find and evaluate information in a text			
		Can respond to and evaluate a text by making explicit references to the text			
Grey (Year 4/P5)	Towards Level 4	Can select different reading styles for different kinds of text			
		Can read aloud with fluency and confidence			
		Can recognize an increasing range of words, including literary language and technical vocabulary			
		Can prepare for reading to find information by identifying what they want to find out and locating relevant sources			
		Can respond critically to issues raised in texts			
		Can review and describe own reading habits			

Progression and planning

Primary Framework objectives chart

The chart below shows the key objectives from the *Primary Framework* that are covered in **Project X** at Grey band in Year 4. Further objectives are covered in the many follow-up activities suggested in the *Guided/Group Reading Notes*.

The following Year 4 framework objective will be supported in every guided/group reading session and is therefore a continuous focus for attention. As you listen to individual children discussing their reading you should undertake ongoing assessment against this objective:

- Interrogate texts to deepen and clarify understanding and response **8.2**

You may also continue to assess children using the following Year 3 objective:

- Use syntax and context to build their store of vocabulary when reading for meaning **7.4**

Book Band and theme	Title	Strands 1–4: Speaking, Listening, Group Interaction and Drama Objectives	Strands 5–8: Reading Objectives
Grey: Dilemmas and Decisions	The Missing Statue	- Tell stories effectively and convey detailed information coherently for listeners **1.3**	- Identify and summarize evidence from a text to support a hypothesis **7.1** - Use knowledge of word structures and origins to develop their understanding of word meanings **7.4**
	Making a Stand	- Create roles showing how behaviour can be interpreted from different viewpoints **4.1**	- Identify and summarize evidence from a text to support a hypothesis **7.1** - Explain how writers use figurative and expressive language to create images and atmosphere **7.5**
	It's Your Call	- Offer reasons and evidence for their views, considering alternative opinions **1.1** - Respond appropriately to the contributions of others in the light of differing viewpoints **1.2**	- Use knowledge of different organizational features of texts to find information effectively **7.3** - Identify and summarize evidence from a text to support a hypothesis **7.1**
	The Witness	- Offer reasons and evidence for their views, considering alternative opinions **1.1** - Respond appropriately to the contributions of others in the light of differing viewpoints **1.2**	- Deduce characters' reasons for behaviour from their actions **7.2** - Explain how writers use figurative and expressive language to create images and atmosphere **7.5**
	A Matter of Life and Death	- Offer reasons and evidence for their views, considering alternative opinions **1.1** - Respond appropriately to the contributions of others in the light of differing viewpoints **1.2**	- Explain how ideas are developed in non-fiction texts **7.2** - Read extensively ... genres and experiment with other types of texts **8.1**

Book Band and theme	Title	Strands 1–4: Speaking, Listening, Group Interaction and Drama Objectives	Strands 5–8: Reading Objectives
Grey: Great Escapes	Revenge of the X-bots	● Develop scripts based on improvisation 4.2	● Identify and summarize evidence from a text to support a hypothesis 7.1 ● Deduce characters' reasons for behaviour from their actions 7.2
	The X-machine	● Create roles showing how behaviour can be interpreted from different viewpoints 4.1	● Identify and summarize evidence from a text to support a hypothesis 7.1 ● Explain how writers use figurative and expressive language to create images and atmosphere 7.5
	Escaping Slavery	● Offer reasons and evidence for their views, considering alternative opinions 1.1 ● Respond appropriately to the contributions of others in the light of differing viewpoints 1.2	● Use knowledge of different organizational features of texts to find information effectively 7.3 ● Identify and summarize evidence from a text to support a hypothesis 7.1
	The Deep	● Compare the different contributions of music, words and images in short extracts from TV programmes 2.2 ● Respond appropriately to the contributions of others in the light of differing viewpoints 1.2	● Explain how writers use figurative and expressive language to create images and atmosphere 7.5
	Escape from Colditz	● Offer reasons and evidence for their views, considering alternative opinions 1.1 ● Respond appropriately to the contributions of others in the light of differing viewpoints 1.2	● Use knowledge of different organizational features of texts to find information effectively 7.3 ● Identify and summarize evidence from a text to support a hypothesis 7.1 ● Read extensively favourite genres and experiment with other types of texts 8.1
Grey: In the News	The WOW! Award	● Offer reasons and evidence for their views, considering alternative opinions 1.1	● Identify and summarize evidence from a text to support a hypothesis 7.1 ● Deduce characters' reasons for behaviour from their actions 7.2
	WOW!	● Offer reasons and evidence for their views, considering alternative opinions 1.1	● Use knowledge of different organizational features of texts to find information effectively 7.3 ● Read different genres and experiment with other types of texts 8.1
	Micro Man Makes Big News	● Respond appropriately to the contributions of others in the light of differing viewpoints 1.2	● Use knowledge of different organizational features of texts to find information effectively 7.3 ● Read extensively ... genres and experiment with other types of texts 8.1
	The Big Story	● Offer reasons and evidence for their views, considering alternative opinions 1.1	● Deduce characters' reasons for behaviour from their actions 7.2
	Making a Splash	● Offer reasons and evidence for their views, considering alternative opinions 1.1 ● Respond appropriately to the contributions of others in the light of differing viewpoints 1.2	● Use knowledge of different organizational features of texts to find information effectively 7.3 ● Identify and summarize evidence from a text to support a hypothesis 7.1 ● Read extensively ... genres and experiment with other types of texts 8.1

Project X and Curriculum for Excellence

Project X has been carefully developed to reflect and support the purposes and principles of the new Scottish curriculum: *Curriculum for Excellence*.

The charts on pages 29-33 show how the English curriculum objectives used in the Year 4/Primary 5 *Guided/Group Reading Notes* correlate to the **Curriculum for Excellence Draft Experiences and Outcomes for Literacy and English**. As the experiences and outcomes are finalised, we will update this correlation.
(See www.OxfordPrimary.co.uk/projectx)

Enjoyment and choice

Recent research by both PISA and the Scottish Survey of Assessment has demonstrated that boys in Scotland are falling behind girls in reading. It also showed that boys are less likely to regard themselves as readers and are less motivated to read. The **Project X** books offer an exciting and motivating choice of content for all your pupils, whilst placing particular emphasis on the needs and tastes of boy readers.

Literacy across the curriculum

The thematic 'cluster' structure of **Project X** supports the application of literacy across the curriculum and provides opportunities for children to learn and apply topic-specific vocabulary. Through its inclusion of cross-curricular activities and links to other subject areas, **Project X** encourages children to develop and apply literacy skills across other curriculum subjects and to become successful learners. The *Guided/Group Reading Notes* provide a range of follow-up activities, many of which are active and hands-on, to support the practical application of literacy skills in a range of contexts. Further ideas for taking this approach to learning are given on pages 58–61 of this Handbook.

A range of text types and ICT opportunities

Project X includes a range of fiction and non-fiction text types and a variety of author styles to ensure that children are exposed to different kinds of text. In addition, the **Project X** *Interactive Stories* software includes interactive electronic versions of some of the core **Project X** stories, giving you the opportunity to embed ICT into your literacy lessons. The *Guided/Group Reading Notes* also provide ICT activities, such as writing an email or using digital photographs to form the basis of a print or ICT text.

Listening and talking

The **Project X** *Guided/Group Reading Notes* place a strong emphasis on the importance of listening and talking both as a precursor to successful reading, comprehension and writing and as a means of ensuring that children become confident individuals and effective contributors. Children are encouraged to talk before, during and after reading, to express preferences and to give and justify their opinions of a book. In addition, there are opportunities for collaborative partner and group work, for giving presentations and for drama activities.

Critical literacy skills

The latest *Curriculum for Excellence* guidance emphasises the importance of critical literacy. The **Project X** *Guided/Group Reading Notes* provide explicit opportunities for the development of comprehension strategies before, during and after reading; encouraging children to read critically and become successful learners.

Assessment is For Learning AiFL / Personalisation

Project X provides extensive assessment support. The *Guided/Group Reading Notes* suggest assessment focuses for reading and listening and talking for every **Project X** book. In addition, there are opportunities to practise self and peer assessment and support for such is provided on pages 44–46 of this Handbook. It should be noted that the wording of the target and assessment focuses can and should be adapted to suit individual learning needs.

Guided/Group Reading

The **Project X** *Guided/Group Reading Notes* provide a model for teachers of how to run a successful guided/group reading session. In line with the latest *Curriculum for Excellence* guidance, **Project X** provides explicit opportunities for the development of reading strategies before, during and after reading. Also included in the *Guided/Group Reading Notes* are a range of follow-up activities to support the link from reading into writing, talking and into other curriculum areas.

Book Band and theme	Title		Objectives used in the Guided/Group Reading Notes	Curriculum for Excellence draft guidelines
Grey: Dilemmas and Decisions	The Missing Statue	Listening and Talking Objectives	• Tell stories effectively and convey detailed information coherently for listeners	• I can select ideas and relevant information, organize these in an appropriate way for my purpose and use suitable vocabulary for my audience **LIT 206F**
		Reading Objectives	• Identify and summarize evidence from a text to support a hypothesis • Use knowledge of word structures and origins to develop their understanding of word meanings	• To show my understanding across different areas of learning, I can identify and consider the purpose and main ideas of my text and use supporting detail **LIT 216S** • Through developing my knowledge of context clues, punctuation, grammar and layout, I can read unfamiliar texts with increasing fluency, understanding and expression **LIT 212N**

Book Band and theme	Title		Objectives used in the Guided/Group Reading Notes	Curriculum for Excellence draft guidelines
Grey: Dilemmas and Decisions	Making a Stand	Listening and Talking Objectives	● Create roles showing how behaviour can be interpreted from different viewpoints	● When I engage with others, I can respond in ways appropriate to my role, show that I value others' contributions and use these to build on thinking **LIT 202B**
		Reading Objectives	● Identify and summarize evidence from a text to support a hypothesis ● Explain how writers use figurative and expressive language to create images and atmosphere	● To show my understanding across different areas of learning, I can identify and consider the purpose and main ideas of my text and use supporting detail **LIT 216S** ● I can discuss the writer's style and other features appropriate to genre **ENG 219V**
	It's Your Call	Listening and Talking Objectives	● Offer reasons and evidence for their views, considering alternative opinions ● Respond appropriately to the contributions of others in the light of differing viewpoints	● To help me develop an informed view, I can distinguish fact from opinion and I am learning to recognize when my sources try to influence me and how useful these are **LIT 208H** ● When I engage with others, I can respond in ways appropriate to my role, show that I value others' contributions and use these to build on thinking **LIT 202B**
		Reading Objectives	● Use knowledge of different organizational features of texts to find information effectively ● Identify and summarize evidence from a text to support a hypothesis	● Using what I know about the features of different types of texts, I can find, select and sort information from a variety of sources and use this for different purposes **LIT 214Q** ● To show my understanding across different areas of learning, I can identify and consider the purpose and main ideas of my text and use supporting detail **LIT 216S**
	The Witness	Listening and Talking Objective	● Offer reasons and evidence for their views, considering alternative opinions ● Respond appropriately to the contributions of others in the light of differing viewpoints	● To help my develop an informed view, I can distinguish fact from opinion and I am learning to recognize when my sources try to influence me and how useful these are **LIT 208H** ● When I engage with others, I can respond in ways appropriate to my role, show that I value others' contributions and use these to build on thinking **LIT 202B**
		Reading Objectives	● Deduce characters' reasons for behaviour from their actions ● Explain how writers use figurative and expressive language to create images and atmosphere	● I can discuss structure, characterization and/or setting **ENG 219V** ● I can discuss the writer's style and other features appropriate to genre **ENG 219V**

Book Band and theme	Title		Objectives used in the Guided/Group Reading Notes	Curriculum for Excellence draft guidelines
Grey: Dilemmas and Decisions	A Matter of Life and Death	**Listening and Talking Objectives**	● Offer reasons and evidence for their views, considering alternative opinions ● Respond appropriately to the contributions of others in the light of differing viewpoints	● To help my develop an informed view, I can distinguish fact from opinion and I am learning to recognize when my sources try to influence me and how useful these are **LIT 208H** ● When I engage with others, I can respond in ways appropriate to my role, show that I value others' contributions and use these to build on thinking **LIT 202B**
		Reading Objectives	● Explain how ideas are developed in non-fiction texts ● Read extensively … genres and experiment	● Using what I know about the features of different types of texts, I can find, select and sort information form a variety of sources and use this for different purposes **LIT 214Q**
Grey: Great Escapes	Revenge of the X-bots	**Listening and Talking Objectives**	● Develop scripts based on improvisation	● I can select ideas and relevant information, organize these in an appropriate way for my purpose and use suitable vocabulary for my audience **LIT 206F**
		Reading Objectives	● Identify and summarize evidence from a text to support a hypothesis ● Deduce characters' reasons for behaviour from their actions	● To show my understanding across different areas of learning, I can identify and consider the purpose and main ideas of my text and use supporting detail **LIT 216S** ● I can discuss structure, characterization and/or setting **ENG 219V**
	The X-machine	**Listening and Talking Objectives**	● Create roles showing how behaviour can be interpreted from different viewpoints	● When I engage with others, I can respond in ways appropriate to my role, show that I value others' contributions and use these to build on thinking LIT 202B
		Reading Objectives	● Identify and summarize evidence from a text to support a hypothesis ● Explain how writers use figurative and expressive language to create images and atmosphere	● To show my understanding across different areas of learning, I can identify and consider the purpose and main ideas of my text and use supporting detail **LIT 216S** ● I can discuss the writer's style and other features appropriate to genre **ENG 219V**
	Escaping Slavery	**Listening and Talking Objectives**	● Offer reasons and evidence for their views, considering alternative opinions ● Respond appropriately to the contributions of others in the light of differing viewpoints	● To help me develop an informed view, I can distinguish fact from opinion and I am learning to recognize when my sources try to influence me and how useful these are **LIT 208H** ● When I engage with others, I can respond in ways appropriate to my role, show that I value others' contributions and use these to build on thinking **LIT 202B**

Book Band and theme	Title		Objectives used in the Guided/Group Reading Notes	Curriculum for Excellence draft guidelines
Grey: Great Escapes	Escaping Slavery	Reading Objectives	● Use knowledge of different organizational features of texts to find information effectively ● Identify and summarize evidence from a text to support a hypothesis	● Using what I know about the features of different types of texts, I can find, select and sort information from a variety of sources and use this for different purposes LIT 214Q ● To show my understanding across different areas of learning, I can identify and consider the purpose and main ideas of my text and use supporting detail LIT 216S
	The Deep	Listening and Talking Objectives	● Compare the different contributions of music, words and images in short extracts from TV programmes ● Respond appropriately to the contributions of others in the light of differing viewpoints	● As I listen or watch, I can use this information for different purposes LIT 204D ● When I engage with others, I can respond in ways appropriate to my role, show that I value others' contributions and use these to build on thinking LIT 202B
		Reading Objectives	● Explain how writers use figurative and expressive language to create images and atmosphere	● I can discuss the writer's style and other features appropriate to genre ENG 219V
	Escape from Colditz	Listening and Talking Objectives	● Offer reasons and evidence for their views, considering alternative opinions ● Respond appropriately to the contributions of others in the light of differing viewpoints	● To help me develop an informed view, I can distinguish fact from opinion and I am learning to recognize when my sources try to influence me and how useful these are LIT 208H ● When I engage with others, I can respond in ways appropriate to my role, show that I value others' contributions and use these to build on thinking LIT 202B
		Reading Objectives	● Use knowledge of different organizational features of texts to find information effectively ● Identify and summarize evidence from a text to support a hypothesis ● Read extensively favourite genres and experiment with other types of texts	● Using what I know about the features of different types of texts, I can find, select and sort information from a variety of sources and use this for different purposes LIT 214Q ● To show my understanding across different areas of learning, I can identify and consider the purpose and main ideas of my text and use supporting detail LIT 216S
Grey: In the News	The WOW! Award	Listening and Talking Objectives	● Offer reasons and evidence for their views, considering alternative opinions	● To help me develop an informed view, I can distinguish fact from opinion and I am learning to recognize when my sources try to influence me and how useful these are LIT 208H
		Reading Objectives	● Identify and summarize evidence from a text to support a hypothesis ● Deduce characters' reasons for behaviour from their actions	● To show my understanding across different areas of learning, I can identify and consider the purpose and main ideas of my text and use supporting detail LIT 216S ● I can discuss structure, characterization and/or setting ENG 219V

Book Band and theme	Title		Objectives used in the Guided/Group Reading Notes	Curriculum for Excellence draft guidelines
Grey: In the News	WOW!	Listening and Talking Objectives	• Offer reasons and evidence for their views, considering alternative opinions	• To help me develop an informed view, I can distinguish fact from opinion and I am learning to recognize when my sources try to influence me and how useful these are **LIT 208H**
		Reading Objectives	• Use knowledge of different organizational features of texts to find information effectively • Read different genres and experiment with other types of texts	• Using what I know about the features of different types of texts, I can find, select and sort information from a variety of sources and use this for different purposes **LIT 214Q**
	Micro Man Makes Big News	Listening and Talking Objectives	• Respond appropriately to the contributions of others in the light of differing viewpoints	• When I engage with others, I can respond in ways appropriate to my role, show that I value others' contributions and use these to build on thinking **LIT 202B**
		Reading Objectives	• Use knowledge of different organizational features of texts to find information effectively • Read extensively … genres and experiment with other types of texts	• Using what I know about the features of different types of texts, I can find, select and sort information from a variety of sources and use this for different purposes **LIT 214Q**
	The Big Story	Listening and Talking Objectives	• Offer reasons and evidence for their views, considering alternative opinions	• To help me develop an informed view, I can distinguish fact from opinion and I am learning to recognize when my sources try to influence me and how useful these are **LIT 208H**
		Reading Objectives	• Deduce characters' reasons for behaviour from their actions	• I can discuss structure, characterization and/or setting **ENG 219V**
	Making a Splash	Listening and Talking Objectives	• Offer reasons and evidence for their views, considering alternative opinions • Respond appropriately to the contributions of others in the light of differing viewpoints	• To help me develop an informed view, I can distinguish fact from opinion and I am learning to recognize when my sources try to influence me and how useful these are **LIT 208H** • When I engage with others, I can respond in ways appropriate to my role, show that I value others' contributions and use these to build on thinking **LIT 202B**
		Reading Objectives	• Use knowledge of different organizational features of texts to find information effectively • Identify and summarize evidence from a text to support a hypothesis • Read extensively … genres and experiment with other types of texts	• Using what I know about the features of different types of texts, I can find, select and sort information from a variety of sources and use this for different purposes **LIT 214Q** • To show my understanding across different areas of learning, I can identify and consider the purpose and main ideas of my text and use supporting detail **LIT 216S**

Project X and the National Curriculum in Wales

Project X has been developed to support the desired English outcomes of the new *National Curriculum for Wales* (2008).

The chart opposite shows how the **Project X** clusters at Year 4 Grey band correlate to the skills and outcomes for Oracy and Reading required by the **Key Stage 2 Programme of Study**.

Talking, communicating and listening

The *National Curriculum for Wales* emphasises the importance of talk and other forms of communication in developing children's literacy and wider social skills. By Key Stage 2, learners are becoming confident, coherent and engaging speakers and active and responsive listeners.

The **Project X** books have been designed to stimulate talk, drama and role play and there is support within the books for exploring characters and settings, raising and responding to questions, and expressing opinions. *The Guided/Group Reading Notes* provide a wealth of opportunities for using talk both as a precursor to successful reading, comprehension and writing, and as a means to ensure that children become confident individuals and effective contributors.

Skills across the curriculum

The new *National Curriculum for Wales* promotes a holistic view of children's learning and encourages the development of skills in a range of contexts. Learners should be given opportunities to build on the skills acquired in the Foundation Phase and continue to acquire, develop, practise, apply and refine these skills as they progress through Key Stage 2.

The thematic 'cluster' structure of **Project X** provides opportunities for children to develop and practise a range of literacy skills – together with broader skills such as thinking and communication – within a familiar context, and then to apply these skills across the curriculum. *The Guided/Group Reading Notes* provide a range of 'after reading' follow-up activities, many of which are active and hands on, to support the application of skills in a range of contexts.

A wide range of print and media experiences

Project X offers children a wide choice of exciting fiction and non-fiction books that are designed to engage all readers, particularly the boys. Children are exposed to different ways of presenting information, are encouraged to 'read the pictures', and supported in making links between different books in the series. The use of digital artwork for the character stories brings the world of modern media to reading books, making them relevant to children whose experiences outside school – even from a very young age – often involved very sophisticated media.

The **Project X** *Interactive Stories* software presents a collection of stories supported by audio and animation, plus links to video clips, images and audio files.

Writing

Throughout **Project X** the importance of linking reading to writing is emphasised. At Key Stage 2, children acquire a broader range of skills and become competent writers across a range of forms and purposes. The **Project X** books at Grey band aim to provide both inspiration for and models of writing to support children's writing development. *The Guided/Group Reading Notes* provide a range of follow-up writing activities from which you can choose the most appropriate for your pupils.

Book Band and Cluster Themes	National Curriculum Level	English Skills	Attainment targets
Grey Band: Dilemmas and Decisions Great Escapes In the News	Working towards Level 4	**Oracy:** ● Listen and view attentively, responding to a wider range of communication ● Identify key points and follow up ideas through question and comment, developing response to others in order to learn through talk ● Communicate clearly and confidently, expressing opinions, adapting talk to audience and purpose ● Use a range of sentence structures and vocabulary ● Evaluate their own and others' talk and drama activities; consider how speakers adapt to a range of situations **Reading:** ● Develop phonic, graphic and grammatical knowledge, word recognition and contextual understanding ● Read with fluency, accuracy, understanding and enjoyment ● Read in different ways for different purposes ● Recognize and understand the characteristics of different genres ● Consider and respond to what they read, selecting evidence from the text to support their views ● Use a range of appropriate information retrieval strategies ● Retrieve and collate information and ideas from a range of sources ● Use knowledge from reading to develop an understanding of vocabulary, grammar and punctuation and how these clarify meaning	**Oracy:** **Level 3** ● Talk and listen confidently in different contexts ● Explore and communicate ideas ● Show an understanding of the main points of a discussion ● Show that they have listened carefully ● Adapt what they say to the needs of the listener ● Express opinions simply and clearly **Level 4** ● Talk and listen confidently in an increasing range of contexts ● Adapt talk to audience and purpose ● Organize ideas, describe events and convey opinions clearly ● Listen carefully, making contributions and asking questions ● Respond to others' ideas and views **Reading:** **Level 3** ● Read a range of texts fluently and accurately ● Use appropriate strategies to read independently and establish meaning ● Show understanding of the main points of a text ● Express opinions and preferences ● Locate books and find information **Level 4** ● Respond to a range of texts showing an understanding of significant themes, ideas, events and characters ● Begin to use inference and deduction ● Refer to the text when expressing views and opinions ● Locate and use ideas and information from more than one source

Project X and the Northern Ireland Primary Curriculum

Project X is fully in line with the aims and objectives of the **Revised Primary Curriculum for Northern Ireland**.

Cross-curricular skills and a thematic approach

The thematic 'cluster' structure of **Project X** supports the application of literacy across the curriculum and provides opportunities for children to learn and apply a range of skills. The structure also helps children to become successful learners – it builds confidence through the familiarity of a theme, supports progression and is highly motivating. The *Guided/Group Reading Notes* provide a range of follow-up activities to support the application of literacy skills in a range of contexts.

Further ideas for taking a thematic approach to learning are given on pages 58-61 of this Handbook.

Engaging pupils in active learning

Project X aims to engage and involve children as readers and as learners. The books themselves are full of action and adventure which is particularly appealing to boys, whilst the *Guided/Group Reading Notes* encourage active learning both during and as a follow-up to group reading sessions. Ideas for drama, talk and things to 'make and do' in response to books are given throughout the programme.

Talking and listening

The importance of talk and other forms of communication in developing children's literacy and wider social skills is widely recognized. The **Project X** books have been designed to stimulate talk and role play and there is support within the books for exploring characters, retelling stories, raising and responding to questions, and expressing opinions. The *Guided/Group Reading Notes* provide a wealth of opportunities for using talk both as a precursor to successful reading, comprehension and writing, and as a means of ensuring that children become confident individuals and effective contributors.

Reading a wide range of texts

Project X offers children a wide choice of exciting fiction and non-fiction books that are designed to engage all readers, particularly the boys. Children are exposed to different ways of presenting information, are encouraged to 'read the pictures', and supported in making links between different books in the series. The use of digital artwork for the character stories brings the world of modern media to reading books, making them relevant to children whose experiences outside school – even from a very young age – often involve very sophisticated media.

The **Project X** *Interactive Stories* software presents a collection of stories supported by audio and animation, plus links to video clips, images and audio files.

Thinking, problem solving and decision making

The character stories within **Project X** present readers with a range of scenarios in which our core characters are faced with problems, challenges and decisions to make. By following the adventures of Max, Cat, Ant and Tiger readers can learn to empathise with situations and explore their own problem solving skills.

Working with others

Throughout **Project X** there is an emphasis on collaborative learning. The *Guided/ Group Reading Notes* provide lots of opportunities for pair and group work linked to talk, reading, drama and writing. Within this Handbook there are also ideas for using peer assessment – see page 40.

Positive attitudes to learning

Project X aims to help all children, particularly the boys, adopt a positive attitude to learning. The highly original and engaging books and software are designed to make all children want to read and to be enthusiastic about the learning process. **Project X** also supports and encourages teachers to have high expectations of all their pupils – something shown to have a powerful impact on young learners.

● Statutory Requirements for Language and Literacy at Key Stage 2

Project X can help you deliver on the following statutory requirements for *Talking and Listening* and *Reading*. It also provides a range of follow-up activities to support children's writing.

Talking and listening

- Listen and respond to a range of fiction, non-fiction and media texts
- Tell, retell and interpret stories based on memories, personal experiences and imagination
- Participate in group discussions – understanding the conventions of group discussion
- Share, respond to and evaluate ideas, arguments and points of view and use evidence or reason to justify opinions
- Participate in a range of drama activities
- Improvise a scene based on experience, imagination, literature, media or curricular topics
- Describe and talk about real or imaginary experiences
- Identify and ask appropriate questions to seek information, views and feelings
- Use appropriate quality of speech – varying according to audience and purpose
- Read aloud, inflecting appropriately, expressing thoughts and feelings and emphasising meaning

Reading

- Participate in modelled, shared, paired and guided reading experiences
- Read, explore, understand and make use of a wide range of texts
- Engage in sustained, independent and silent reading for enjoyment and information
- Extend their range of reading and develop preferences
- Use books to locate, select and evaluate information
- Consider, interpret and discuss texts, exploring the ways in which language creates effect or engages attention
- Justify responses to texts using inference, deduction and/or with reference to evidence in text
- Read aloud, using inflection to assist meaning
- Use a range of cross-checking strategies to read unfamiliar words
- Use a variety of reading skills for different reading purposes

Assessing Pupils' Progress

Approaches to assessment

Teachers constantly assess pupils by observing what they can do, what they struggle with and what they can't do. Evidence of achievement is collected in a variety of ways and then evaluated. Finally teachers (and sometimes children) form a judgement on the basis of that evidence. Such assessment processes are an everyday part of classroom practice and should involve both teachers and learners in reflection, dialogue and decision-making.

Sometimes judgements are used for summative assessment purposes – to 'sum up' what a child can do at a given point in time. Others are used for formative assessment purposes – for learners and their teachers to decide where the learners are in their learning, where they need to go and how best to get there. These two purposes of assessment are often described as assessment of learning and assessment for learning.

Assessment for learning opportunities are fully integrated into the guided/group reading sessions in **Project X**. Clearly identified 'child speak' targets (directly related to the teaching objectives) are given to ensure that both the learner and the teacher understand what is to be learnt. Assessing against the target provides opportunities for both learner and teacher to comment and reflect on progress towards the learning goal/s. If they know their learning goal and how it will be assessed children can be involved in self assessment and peer assessment. Teachers should give feedback against the targets; discuss what they have achieved in relation to the target and what they should do next to progress in their learning. Giving positive feedback against targets helps focus on the work rather than the person which is more constructive for both learning and motivation. Assessment for learning information feeds back into the planning process (what does the child need to do next?).

Using Assessment Focuses

The assessment for learning opportunities within the guided/group reading sessions are linked to the reading assessment focuses (AFs) that inform the National Curriculum levels for English. This means the evidence gathered during these assessment opportunities can also feed into a structured approach to *periodically* assessing reading against national criteria. This approach is currently being promoted by the Primary National Strategy and QCA in *Assessing Pupil Progress* (APP).

An assessment approach based on AFs enables you to build a detailed profile of what the child can do in relation to the AFs. From this you can assign an evidence-based National Curriculum level for each child based on an informed holistic judgement rather than relying solely on tests and tasks. You can track pupils' progress through the levels and use diagnostic information about their strengths and weaknesses to inform planning. Many Year 4 teachers are already skilled in judging their children's work against AFs and assign a National Curriculum level based on both the summative assessment evidence of the national tests and periodic assessments made within a curriculum context. **Project X** helps you build this into your guided/group reading sessions.

The AF chart on page 39 shows the detailed elements of each reading assessment focus so that you can match the qualities you have noted in a child's work against these criteria. The chart can be used to inform and record your judgements against specific assessment focuses and extrapolate these to accurately assess a pupil's National Curriculum level.

Pupil Name.................... Class/Group.................... Date.............

	AF2 – understand, describe, select or retrieve information, events or ideas from texts and use quotation and reference to text	AF3 – deduce, infer or interpret information, events or ideas from text	AF4 – identify and comment on the structure and organization of texts, including grammatical and presentational features at text level	AF5 – explain and comment on writers' use of language, including grammatical and literary features at word and sentence level	AF6 – identify and comment on writers' purposes and viewpoints, and the overall effect of the text on the reader	AF7 – relate texts to their social, cultural and historical traditions
Level 4	**Across a range of reading** • some relevant points identified • comments supported by some generally relevant textual reference or quotation, e.g. reference is made to appropriate section of text but is unselective and lacks focus	**Across a range of reading** • comments make inferences based on evidence from different points in the text, e.g. interpreting character's motive from their actions at different points • inferences are often correct, but comments are not always rooted securely in the text or repeat narrative or content	**Across a range of reading** • some structural choices identified with simple comment, e.g. 'he describes the accident first and then goes back to tell you why the child was in the road' • some basic features of organization at text level identified, e.g. 'the writer uses bullet points for the main reasons'	**Across a range of reading** • some basic features of writer's use of language identified, e.g. 'all the questions make you want to find out what happens next' • simple comments of writer's choices, e.g. '"disgraceful" is a good word to use to show he is upset'	**Across a range of reading** • main purpose identified, e.g. 'it's all about why going to the dentist is important and how you should look after your teeth' • simple comments show some awareness of writer's viewpoint, e.g. 'he only tells you good things about the farm and makes the shop sound boring' • simple comment on overall effect on the reader, e.g. 'the way she describes him as "ratlike" and "shifty" makes you think he's disgusting'	**Across a range of reading** • features common to different texts or versions of the same text identified, with simple comment, e.g. characters, settings and presentational features • simple comment on the effect that the reader's or writer's context has on the meaning of texts, e.g. historical context, place, social relationships
Level 3	**In most reading** • simple, most obvious points identified though there may also be some misunderstanding, e.g. about information from different places in the text • some comments include quotations from or references to text, but not always relevant, e.g. often retelling or paraphrasing sections of that text rather than using it to support comment	**In most reading** • straightforward inference based on a single point of reference in the text, e.g. 'he was upset because it says "he was crying"' • responses to text show meaning established at a literal level e.g. "walking good" means "walking carefully" or based on personal speculation e.g. a response based on what they personally would be feeling rather than feelings of character in the text	**In most reading** • a few basic features of organization at text level identified, with little or no linked comment, e.g. 'it tells about all the different things you can do at the zoo'	**In most reading** • a few basic features of writer's use of language identified, but with little or no comments, e.g. 'there are lots of adjectives' or 'he uses speech marks to show there are lots of people there'	**In most reading** • comments identify main purpose, e.g. 'the writer doesn't like violence' • express personal response but with little awareness of writer's viewpoint or effect on reader, e.g. 'she was just horrible like my nan is sometimes'	**In most reading** • some simple connections between texts identified, e.g. similarities in plot, topic, or books by same author, about same characters • recognitions of some features of the context of texts, e.g. historical setting, social or cultural background
BL						
IE						

Key: BL – Below Level   IE – Insufficient Evidence

Overall assessment (tick one box only)

☐ Low 2   ☐ Secure 2   ☐ High 2   ☐ Low 3   ☐ Secure 3   ☐ High 3

© Crown copyright 2008

Assessing and recording against targets

Turning objectives into clear, child-relevant targets and sharing these targets with the learner enables children to understand the focus for their learning. It also helps to engage children in reflecting on whether they have achieved their goals and made progress. This is particularly important to boys, who need to see a clear purpose for their learning and clear evidence of their own success.

Within the **Project X** *Guided/Group Reading Notes* are speaking and listening and reading targets related to the teaching objectives. On the following pages, you will find photocopiable assessment sheets for each cluster of books. These can be used for group or individual assessment against the targets. The assessment can be done during a guided/group reading session as you listen to individual children read and observe their participation in and understanding of the pre- and post-reading activities.

Self and peer assessment

Encouraging learners to self evaluate and to become involved in positive assessment of their peers is an important part of assessment for learning. It encourages learners to reflect on their targets and judge themselves against criteria relevant to the target. This helps them understand that assessment is not an arbitrary process. It also helps them become self aware and self critical. They develop an understanding that assessment can help them see how to improve by focusing on what they have done well and where/how they can get better.

On pages 44–46 you will find a series of photocopiable self assessment sheets so that children can record and track their own progress against their reading targets for each cluster at Grey band. These sheets can also be used for peer-assessment. The self assessment sheets can be stuck in the front of children's literacy books or reading diaries and children encouraged to self assess against one or two of the reading targets each week. What to record on their self assessment sheet should result from a discussion with an adult or a reading partner, following a reading session.

Assessing and recording comprehension skills

The *Guided/Group Reading Notes* that accompany the **Project X** books identify the comprehension strategies that are being developed as readers undertake various activities before, during and after reading. The comprehension assessment chart (see page 47) can be used at regular intervals – for example, on completion of a cluster of books or every half term – to assess the comprehension skills of the guided group reading group or of individual children. This chart will enable you to see at a glance those skills which are well established and those that require further support.

In future sessions, you can then select the appropriate activities from the many comprehension opportunities suggested in the *Guided/Group Reading Notes*, to support the skills needing further development.

The comprehension assessment chart also allows teachers to record whether learners are developing the metacognitive skills of identifying an appropriate strategy to use and assessing its effectiveness.

PROJECT X – Guided reading targets and assessment record
GREY BAND: DILEMMAS AND DECISIONS

Book	Reading target We can ...	Name of child or group:			
		HIGH	SECURE	LOW	Comments
The Missing Statue Date	Enact and retell the story we have read **AF2/3**				
	Identify clues to a character's personality and justify our ideas with evidence from the text **AF2/3**				
	Answer questions and discuss what we have read **AF2/3**				
	Identify vocabulary on the theme of detection and say what the words mean **AF2**				
Making a Stand Date	Role play Dr X showing different aspects of his life and character, using appropriate language **AF2/3**				
	Identify clues to a character's personality and justify our ideas with evidence from the text **AF2/3**				
	Answer questions and discuss what we have read **AF2/3**				
	Identify how language is used to create images atmosphere **AF2/5**				
It's Your Call Date	Debate issues and reach a decision, listening to and responding to different views **AF2/3**				
	Locate information efficiently and use it to support our ideas **AF2**				
The Witness Date	Debate decisions, listening to and responding to different views on these **AF3**				
	Explain what character's actions tell us about their character **AF3**				
	Identify where authors have used special language and explain its impact **AF5**				
A Matter of Life and Death Date	Debate decisions, listening to and responding to different views on these **AF3**				
	Explain how ideas are developed in non-fiction texts **AF2**				
	Read and recognize a range of genres including mixed genre texts **AF4**				

PROJECT X – Guided reading targets and assessment record
GREY BAND: GREAT ESCAPES

Book	Reading targets We can ...	Name of child or group:			
		HIGH	SECURE	LOW	Comments
Revenge of the X-bots **Date**	Perform playscripts based on a story and say how they affect the reader **AF2/6**				
	Identify clues to a character's emotions and justify our ideas with evidence from the text **AF2/3**				
	Use role play to help us understand what we have read **AF2/3**				
The X-Machine **Date**	Role play Dr X and other characters, showing different aspects of their characters and using appropriate language **AF2/3**				
	Identify clues to a character's personality and justify our ideas with evidence from the text **AF2/3**				
	Comment on the writer's use of language **AF5**				
Escaping Slavery **Date**	Debate issues and reach a decision, listening to and responding to different views **AF2/3**				
	Locate information efficiently and use it to support our ideas **AF2**				
	Show understanding of a text and give personal responses to it **AF2/3**				
The Deep **Date**	Discuss and compare the effect of language in different texts **AF5**				
	Debate issues and reach a decision, listening to and responding to different views **AF2/3**				
	Show understanding of a text and give personal responses to it **AF2/3**				
	Talk about the impact of the author's use of language on the reader **AF5**				
Escape from Colditz **Date**	Debate issues and reach a decision, listening to and responding to different views **AF2/3**				
	Locate information efficiently and use it to support our ideas **AF2**				
	Read and recognize a range of genres including mixed range genres **AF4**				

PROJECT X – Guided reading targets and assessment record
GREY BAND: IN THE NEWS

Book	Reading targets We can ...	Name of child or group:			
		HIGH	SECURE	LOW	Comments
The WOW! Award **Date**	Reflect on ideas that people contribute to a discussion **AF3**				
	Identify clues to a character's personality and feelings and justify our ideas with evidence from the text **AF2/3**				
	Answer questions and discuss what we have read **AF2/3**				
WOW! **Date**	Express personal preferences and give reasons for them **AF6**				
	Read more efficiently by understanding organizational features of non-fiction texts, including the layout of a page or spread **AF4**				
	Recognize the language styles an author uses for different genres **AF5**				
Micro Man Makes Big News **Date**	Debate issues and reach a decision, listening to and responding to different views **AF2/3**				
	Locate information efficiently and use it to support our ideas **AF2**				
	Read and recognize a range of genres and give our preferences **AF4**				
The Big Story **Date**	Use visual and written evidence to infer what is not said explicitly in the text **AF2/3**				
	Talk about why characters behave in different ways **AF3**				
	Show some understanding of a writer's viewpoint **AF6**				
Making a Splash **Date**	Debate issues and reach a decision, listening to and responding to different views **AF2/3**				
	Locate information efficiently and use it to support our ideas **AF2**				
	Read and recognize a range of genres including mixed genre texts **AF4**				

Project X – Self assessment sheet: Grey band – Dilemmas and Decisions

Name	
My reading targets	
I can answer questions and discuss what I have read	
I can identify clues to a character's personality and justify my ideas with evidence from the text	
I can explain what a character's actions tell us about their character	
I can talk about how language is used to create images and atmosphere	
I can show where authors have used special language and explain its impact	
I can identify new topic words and say what the words mean	
I can find information in a text and use it to support my ideas	

Project X – Self assessment sheet: Grey band – Great Escapes

Name	
My reading targets	
I can identify clues to a character's emotions and justify my ideas with evidence from the text	
I can use role play to present or explore what I have read	
I can talk about the writer's use of language	
I can talk about issues with others and respond to their views	
I can find information in a text and use it to support my ideas	
I can show that I understand a text and say what I think about it and why	
I can read and recognize a range of genres including mixed genre texts	

Project X – Self assessment sheet: Grey band – In the News

Name	
My reading targets	
I can answer questions and discuss what I have read	
I can talk about how characters behave and why, using evidence from the text	
I can talk about a text, saying what I think about it and why	
I can understand the organization of a non-fiction text and use it to help find information	
I can recognize the different language styles that different authors use	
I can infer meaning from a text	
I can understand the writer's point of view	
I can read and recognize a range of genres including mixed genre texts	

Comprehension Assessment Chart

This chart can be used at any point to assess the comprehension skills of a group or of an individual child.

√ = skills secure   / = not yet secure, more experience required

Name of child or group :	Dates:					
Comprehension Skill						
Uses prior knowledge						
Makes sensible predictions						
Supports predictions with evidence						
Confirms/changes predictions in the light of further reading						
Asks own questions of text						
Clarifies unknown vocabulary/phrases/sentences						
Uses visualization techniques to enhance understanding						
Uses other sensory techniques to enhance understanding						
Retells sequentially						
Retells in detail						
Makes inferences from text/illustrations						
Can deduce implicit information						
Can synthesize separate information						
Can summarize main points of story/information text						
Identifies relevant/irrelevant material (determining importance)						
Identifies what has been learned						
Distinguishes between fact and opinion						
Draws conclusions						
Can empathize with characters/behaviours						
Discusses author's point of view						
Discusses author's intentions						
Can take a critical stance to the text						
Makes personal responses						
Supports views with evidence from the text						
Reflection on Learning						
Can identify strategies used						
Can reflect on the effectiveness of strategies in supporting their understanding						

Reading Partners

Opportunities to read to a reading partner who has a similar reading ability can encourage children to share their success as a reader and undertake joint problem solving when they encounter difficulties. As the 'listener' has to follow the text as well, they too are practising their reading skills.

Reading partners should be encouraged to discuss the books they share – what they thought of them, what they learned, and any questions they have. This will help build a culture in which children see reading as a social and pleasurable activity. You could also encourage reading partners to share some of their discussion with the rest of the class.

You will need to model reading partner practice and talk through the prompt sheet [see page 49] before launching reading partnerships. Children should have a copy of the prompt sheet or you could enlarge it to A3 poster size and display.

Celebrating Achievement

With such an emphasis on targets and assessment it is important to children – as with any learner – that success is recognized and celebrated. Ongoing and informal praise of children's achievement is a key part of good teaching practice and guided or group reading sessions are an ideal time to focus on individual children. Children should also be encouraged to praise their peers and to identify and celebrate their own success.

On pages 50-51 you will find reading and writing certificate templates, featuring the **Project X** characters. These can be used to celebrate the success of individuals or groups at any point in the school year.

Reading and Listening Partner Prompts

Before reading

Reader and listener:

- Look at the book together
- Talk about what you think it will be about

During reading

Listener:

- Listen really carefully
- Help your partner if they get stuck on a word

After reading

Reader and listener:

- Tell each other what you thought of the book
- What did you learn?
- What questions do you have?

Listener:

Tell your partner what you liked about their reading.

- Did they read with expression?
- Did they 'have a go' at hard words?

Reader and listener:

Decide if the reading was

- Fantastic
- Good
- A good try but need to practise and read again

Certificate for GREAT reading

has been awarded this certificate for

WELL DONE!

Max Cat Ant Tiger

Signed:

Date:

Certificate for GREAT writing

has been awarded this certificate for

WELL DONE!

Signed: Max Cat Ant Tiger

Date:

Running Records

During your ongoing assessments of pupils you may identify a child who is falling behind their peers or who is failing to make progress at a particular point in time. Such children need a detailed, individual assessment of their reading strengths and weaknesses in order that you can identify the action needed to bring them back on track. A running record is a useful way to assess a child's reading strengths, areas for development, accuracy rate, error rate and self-correction rate.

As well as using running records to assess individual children at a point of specific need, they can also be used as regular progress checks. In particular, they are a useful way of helping you to assess and place children in appropriate guided reading groups.

Using the running record

Running records should be conducted with 'unseen' texts, so that they are a true assessment of a child's ability to read and interpret a new text. You can use any book at the appropriate level to undertake a running record. However on the following pages you will find a running record sample from a **Project X** book at Grey Band. If you choose to use this text, you need to be aware of the sample given and ensure you use it to undertake a running record before the child you wish to assess has encountered the text in a guided/group reading session.

You will need:

- A copy of the appropriate running record recording sheet for the approximate reading level of the child - there is one sheet for Grey Band on page 55, although you may create others if you wish
- A copy of the book for the child to read from as you record
- A quiet space in which to conduct the assessment.

Before reading

- Explain to the child that you want to find out what they are doing well in their reading and where they might need a little bit more help. Stress that this is not a 'test'. Explain that you will be making some notes as they read so that you both can see what they did.
- Ask the child to read the piece of text aloud to you.

During reading

- Mark up your copy of the text as the child reads using the conventions shown on the reading behaviours chart opposite.
- Indicate whether the child used meaning/context (M), decoding (ph), structure/syntax (S) or visual cues (V) in working out new or unfamiliar words.
- Also record what strategies the child used in self-correcting errors.
- If the child struggles with a word give them plenty of time to try out different ways of identifying the word. Avoid the temptation to instantly prompt them as you want to assess what the child can do unaided. When it is clear that the child is not going to read the word unaided you can then offer prompts or give the word.

After reading

- Give the child some immediate positive feedback e.g. look, here you said the wrong word but you realized it was wrong and then you corrected the mistake. Well done.
- Ask the child to summarize what they have read and ask them a few questions to informally assess their overall understanding. Include questions that require recall, inference and deduction.

Running Records – Reading Behaviours Chart

Child's reading behaviour	How to record	Example
Child reads accurately (no error)	√ Tick each correct word	√ √ √ √ √ Every cloud has a silver
Child substitutes another word (counts as one error even if several different words tried)	Write final substituted word above the word	√ car √ √ √ Every cloud has a silver
Child self-corrected substitution (no error)	Write SC after substitution to indicate self-corrected	√ car/SC √ √ √ Every cloud has a silver
Child omits a word (one error)	Write a long dash above the word	√ √ √ – √ Every cloud has a silver
Child inserts a word (one error)	Write ^ at point of insertion and the word inserted	√ little √ √ √ √ Every ^ cloud has a silver
Child corrects repetition of a word or phrase (no error)	Write R1 (one repetition), R2 (two repetitions) etc above word. If a phrase is repeated underline the phrase.	√ R2 √ √ √ Every cloud has a silver
Child sounds out all or part of a word (no error if correct; one error if word given by teacher)	Mark the sounds used and write √ if word correct or G if word given	√ c l /ow/d√ √ √ √ Every cloud has a silver
Teacher prompting: Child stops after one attempt and does not try again – teacher prompts them to have another go (one error)	Write TP above the word then √ if word read correctly or G if word then given	√ TP√ √ √ √ Every cloud has a silver √ TP/G √ √ √ Every cloud has a silver
Teacher intervention: Child makes no attempt to read the word (one error)	Write G above the word if child is given the word after a 5-10 second wait	√ G √ √ √ Every cloud has a silver

Analysing the running record

It is best to undertake the detailed analysis of a running record immediately after a session while it is still fresh in your mind.

Your analysis should follow this basic format:

1. Note your general comments about the child's reading and understanding of the text.
2. Note the number of errors and self-corrections.
3. Look at the types of cues and strategies the child used during errors and self correcting:
   - Are they over-dependent on one particular cue?
   - Are there any cues they are not using?
   - Was the child confident to attempt words they were finding difficult?
   - Is there any repeated pattern of errors e.g. a particular word/phoneme?
4. Reflect on what this tells you about the child's strengths and areas for development.
5. Note the child's specific needs and ideas for further experiences in the next steps box.

Numerical analysis

You may also wish to undertake a numerical analysis of the running record using the first 100 words of the sample text, as follows:

Self-correction rate

A child's self-correction rate is expressed as a ratio and is calculated using the following formula:

$$\frac{(E + SC)}{SC} = SC \text{ rate} \qquad \frac{(\text{Errors} + \text{self-corrections})}{\text{self-corrections}} = \text{self-correction rate}$$

Example:

$$\frac{(10 + 5)}{5} = SC \qquad \frac{15}{5} = SC \qquad 3 = SC$$

The SC rate is 1:3. This means that the child corrects 1 out of every 3 errors.

If a child has a self-correcting rate of 1:3 or less, this indicates that they are successfully self-monitoring their reading. A higher ratio (1:4 and above) indicates that the child needs more support in reading for meaning.

Accuracy rate

A child's accuracy rate is expressed as a percentage and is calculated using the following formula:

$$\frac{(\text{Total words read} - \text{total errors})}{\text{Total words read}} \times 100 = \text{Accuracy rate}$$

Example:

$$\frac{(110 - 6)}{110} \times 100 = AR \qquad \frac{104}{110} \times 100 = AR \qquad 94\% = AR$$

The accuracy rate indicates the level of difficulty of the text for the reader as follows:

Accuracy Rate	Text level
95–100%	Easy enough for independent reading
90–94%	Guided reading instructional level
Below 90%	Too difficult – frustration level for independent reading

Running record sheet

Name of child:	BOOK BAND 13: GREY
	BOOK TITLE: THE WITNESS
Date:	

Symbols:

√ = correct   SC = self-corrected   − = word omitted

^ = word inserted   TP = Teacher prompt   G = given

Strategies used:

M = meaning (context)   V = visual   Ph = decoding   S = structure/syntax

As you mark up the text you should assess the strategy the child uses e.g. self-correcting may involve using meaning or sentence structure or both. If two strategies are used together enclose these in a circle.

	Type of strategy
At afternoon break it was raining and so we had to stay in the classroom. I had to go to the book corner and Barry said, "Did you say anything, Slow Eddie?" I said, "No way!" So Gary said, "Nice one." Then he said to meet them at the gate after school. "We've got something for you." After school I tried to be really quick. I put my jacket on even before the bell went because I said I was cold. Miss Hicks said I didn't look cold, I looked sweaty. Then Mr Rose, who is our head teacher and is called Rambling Rose because he talks a lot, asked me to help him carry some books to the library. Total words: 120	

General comment on reading and understanding

Use of reading cues

Self-correction rate

Accuracy rate

Next steps

Reading at home – working with parents/carers

Parents and/or carers are children's first and continuing teachers. It is well known that parents who regularly read with and to their children, and who act as good 'model readers' themselves, play a vital role in children's development as readers. A home or care situation in which a wide variety of reading material – books, magazines, newspapers, the internet, and so on – is seen and valued as a part of every day life makes a huge difference to children's attitudes to reading.

Of course, not all home backgrounds provide these 'ideal' conditions. Some parents/carers may need your support to become actively involved in helping their child understand the pleasures and purposes of reading. It is important, too, to be sensitive to those parents/carers for whom English is not a first language (or indeed, where English isn't spoken at all) or who may struggle with literacy themselves.

By Year 4/P5 many parents may have given up on reading to or with their children.
It is important to help them understand that it is worth continuing to do these things even when their child is beyond the beginning reader stage.

Your approach to parent or carer needs will, to some extent, depend on your individual school situation. But whatever the circumstances, the vast majority of parents do want to help their children learn and there are many exciting and innovative ways schools can encourage this. You could, for example:

- Have reading induction meetings where you explain how parents/carers can help with reading, role play 'hearing a child read' and show a range of literacy resources that involve enjoyable reading activities.
- Offer parents, or loan out to parents, the NIACE/Basic Skills Agency family literacy resources such as *Read and Write Together*, *Learning with Grandparents*, *Fun at home*, *Fun outdoors* and so on. See http://archive.basic-skills.co.uk/
- Involve children and parents/carers in national projects such as Dads and Lads, Reading Champions, Family Learning Week and so on.
- Arrange special family induction trips to the local library or arrange for the mobile library to come to the school playground once a week.
- Involve parents/carers in creating Story Sacks and Curiosity Kits – fiction and non-fiction book bags with related artefacts and toys – to use in the home.
- Have a library of reading games that can be taken home to play.
- Have family quiz events to generate discussion and enthusiasm around reading, or create a supermarket word trail.
- Involve parents/carers in celebrating events such as World Book Day, Children's Book Week, National Storytelling Week, National Poetry Day and so on.
- Run your own book awards event and have parent/carer votes as well as children's.
- Run a regular 'book swap' stall where both parents and children can swap books, comics and magazines.

Inside the cover of each **Project X** book are notes for parents/carers that point out tricky vocabulary, encourage talk about books, and suggest some fun activities that parents/carers and children can enjoy together.

Opposite you will find a sheet of simple tips and practical advice for parents/carers on how to support their child with their reading. This can be photocopied or adapted for your own Home-School programme.

Reading with your child

Here are some simple tips to help you help your child with reading

Enjoy it!

- Make book sharing a fun time that you both enjoy – snuggle up with a book!
- When your child reads to you, show them that you are proud of what they can do.
- Even though your child can now read it's still important that you read to them to help them develop into enthusiastic readers. Read them old favourites – even if they do seem 'easy' – as well as longer or harder books that they can't manage themselves.
- If you have a shared interest or hobby, look at books and magazines on the topic together.

Make time and space!

- Make reading a special part of your day. Try to find a time when you aren't busy doing other things so you can spend 'quality time' reading together – even if it's only for a few minutes.
- Try to find a quiet place away from distractions like the television or the computer.
- Try to find some time every week for reading together.
- If your child is reluctant to read you could offer a small reward such as playing a game they enjoy. If they are tired or very reluctant to read to you, read to them instead. Don't force them.

Be positive!

- Give your child lots praise, encouragement and support when they read to you. Focus on what they did well, not what they did wrong. Even small successes are important.

Find out what they like to read!

- Sometimes we read for pleasure but most of the time we read for a reason. Read lots of different things together – stories, information books, comics, magazines, websites, cereal packets, TV listings – anything you and your child enjoy reading or need to read.
- Let your child make his or her own reading choices sometimes. They need to develop their own personal likes and dislikes. It is OK not to like some books! Don't worry if they choose an 'easy' or favourite book sometimes. This is normal and helps children build their reading confidence and enthusiasm.
- Join the local library and let your child choose from the great range of books on offer.

Talk about it!

- Talking about books helps your child become more involved and interested in reading and can help them understand more.
- Discuss what your child has read and what they think about it. Encourage them to develop their own ideas and tastes - it's OK *not* to like some books! This will help your child become a lifelong reader.
- You can talk with your child about anything – games, TV programmes, films or other things you do together.

Project X – Using a thematic approach

Over the last few years more and more primary schools have begun to move away from teaching all curriculum subjects in separate slots in the timetable to one where some subjects are linked together in cross-curricular 'themes'. The Primary National Strategy, through various initiatives, has supported this approach, while stressing that links should be strong and meaningful, not tenuous.

Making links between curriculum subjects can deepen children's understanding by providing opportunities to enhance their learning. It does this in a number of ways.

- It mirrors the way we learn 'naturally', outside school – our learning environment is often holistic, for example, going shopping might involve literacy, maths and geography.
- It builds and enriches concepts – by presenting the same or related information in different ways, through different modes of communication or within different contexts.
- It provides opportunities for the application of knowledge within familiar, new and related contexts and supports children in using higher order thinking skills such as reasoning and problem solving.
- It provides opportunities for practising skills – so, skills taught in one curriculum area (e.g. skimming, scanning and analyzing data in literacy) can be developed through purposeful use in other areas such as history or science.
- It helps children retain their learning through the repetition of information, actions and skills in different contexts.
- It makes learning enjoyable – cross-curricular learning often feels more meaningful and more fun, so motivation and engagement can be enhanced.

In using cross-curricular themes it is important to recognize that planning is still usually undertaken at subject level to ensure curriculum coverage and continuity. For this reason the cross-curricular potential of the themes in **Project X** are linked to the National Curriculum Programmes of Study. The grids on pages 59-61 contain suggestions for many activities linked to the wider curriculum, as well as ideas for creating a contextualised learning environment which will encourage children to make their own explorations of a theme through play and other activities. Such activities also encourage them to make direct links between the theme and their own knowledge and experiences.

At each Book Band level **Project X** offers five books linked by a theme. This cluster structure is designed to support a cross-curricular approach and to be motivating and engaging for readers.

Project X-Grey Band-
Theme: Great Escapes

Cross-curricular opportunities – Theme: Dilemmas and Decisions

The learning environment

- Have a range of games or other stimulations that require children to make decisions. These can be ICT based or paper based.
- You could create an emergencies command post with lists of dilemmas for children to resolve. Have different modes of communicating, e.g. phones, computers, note pads, incident sheets, report forms etc.
- Ensure there are plenty of story books and non-fiction materials – including multi media materials – involving people having to make difficult choices. These can involve both physical and moral dilemmas.

National Curriculum subject	Programme of study	Suggested activities
Mathematics	*MA 2 Using and applying number* *4 Solving numerical problems* *a) problems involving 'real life'... money*	Devise problems involving a dilemma and money – e.g. provide an equipment price list and set budget to spend in a situation such as an expedition. Include essential and non-essential items for children to make choices from. (Link to *A Matter of Life and Death*) Create dice games involving choices. (Link to *The Witness* and *The Mystery of the Missing Statue*)
Science / ICT	*Sc3 Materials and their properties* *b) that some materials are better thermal insulators than others*	Explore the waterproofing and thermal properties of materials through a series of fair tests. Record results using ICT and draw conclusions. Discuss which materials would be best suited for use at sea or in freezing conditions. (Link to *A Matter of Life and Death*)
Geography/ PHSE/ Citizenship	*5 Knowledge and understanding of environmental change* *a) how people can improve/ damage the environment* *2 Preparing to play a role as active citizens* *a) research and discuss topical issues, problems and events; make real choices and decisions*	Explore issues such as traffic/travel, uses of water, recycling or other relevant issues in the locality/ school. Look at the decisions and dilemmas involved in these issues. (Link to *It's Your Call*)
Art and design/ ICT	*4 Knowledge and understanding* *a) Visual and tactile elements including colour, pattern and texture, line and tone, shape, form and space, and how these elements are combined and organized for different purposes*	Look at leaflets and posters about energy saving/ recycling. Explore how images and graphics are used to put across a message. Using photographs and graphics, create your own posters or leaflets to show how to make a difference to the environment. (Link to *It's Your Call*)
History	*2 Knowledge and understanding of events* *c) identify and describe reasons for and results of historical events* *5 Organization and communication* *c) communicate their knowledge of history in a variety of ways*	Undertake further research into one of the events outlined in *A Matter of Life and Death*. Devise a cause/effect sequential flowchart detailing the events researched. (Link to *A Matter of Life and Death*)
PHSE	*4 Developing good relationships* *d) to realise the nature and consequences of bullying, how to respond and how to ask for help.*	Discuss bullying and how to combat it; enact some bullying scenarios and possible reactions. Draw up a 'Say no to Bullying' protocol (Link to *The Witness*) Discuss being decisive and brave in difficult circumstances. (link to *Making a Stand*)

Cross-curricular opportunities – Theme: Great Escapes

The learning environment

- Small world or other play opportunities could include underwater worlds and submarines/submersibles.
- Create a role play area in the form of an escape-planning group meeting place. Have plans of buildings, maps, atlases, equipment for making fake 'papers' etc
- Create or provide indoor and outdoor games that involve chasing/escaping.
- Provide books, DVDs and other materials on a range of famous escapes such as escapologists, famous escapees, and rescue vehicles/equipment.
- Arrange a visit from one of the emergency services involved in rescuing people in danger such as the fire brigade or a lifeboat crew.

National Curriculum subject	Programme of study	Suggested activities
Mathematics	*MA3 space, shape and measures* 3) Understanding properties of position and movement	Plot coordinates for an escape route on a map of a compound or a seascape with many hazards, or link to the fictional NASTI setting. (Link to *Escape from Colditz*, *The Deep* or *The X-Machine*)
Geography/ History	*Geographical skills* c) Use atlases, maps and plans *11. Britain since the 1930s*	Research POW escapes in WW2. Map the escape routes onto a map of Europe (Link to *Escape from Colditz*)
Art and design	*5 Breadth of study* Using a range of materials and processes	Create a wanted poster for a famous escapee – either real or fictional. (Link to *The X-machine*, *Escaping Slavery*, *Escape from Colditz*)
Music	*1 Controlling sounds through singing and playing* a) Use their voice expressively by singing songs	Research, rehearse and sing some slave songs from North America. (Link to *Escaping Slavery*)
ICT	*2) Developing ideas and making things happen* c) to use simulations	Undertake the escaping slave simulation exercise on the National Geographic Underground Railroad site *http://www. nationalgeographic.com/railroad/j1.html* (Link to *Escaping Slavery*)
D/T	*Breadth of study* Design and make assignments using a range of materials. All processes a-d	Create a suitcase from scrap material for use in an escape. Also create authentic looking papers, using a restricted range of materials and printing equipment, for the escapee to use. (Link to *Escape from Colditz*)
PSHE/ citizenship	*2 Playing an active role as citizens* a) to take part in discussions	Discuss why people attempt to escape from imprisonment and oppression. Relate to some modern day refugees and the journeys some of them undertake.

Cross-curricular opportunities – Theme: In the News

The learning environment

- You could set up a newspaper or magazine 'office'. Provide a range of reading and writing materials, including a computer/printer etc if possible, so that children can source and create pieces for the newspaper or magazine.
- Ensure there are a range of newspapers (local, national and international) and magazines available for children to review, plus audio, video and internet sources of news. (There are a range of sources designed specially for children, such as www.bbc.co.uk/cbbcnews)
- Provide a range of story and non-fiction books relating to the theme of news.
- Arrange a visit from a local reporter or a visit to a local newspaper.

National Curriculum subject	Programme of study	Suggested activities
Mathematics	*MA 3 Handling Data* 2c) processing and interpreting data; represent and interpret discrete data using graphs, pictograms and bar charts	Analyse TV listing timetables and process the data to show the amount of airtime given to different categories of broadcasting, including news programmes. Compare results across the four main TV channels.
Science	*Breadth of Study* c) use a range of information sources and data	Using whatever science topic you are covering, ask children to research, write and prepare a live 'science correspondent' broadcast. You can then video and/or podcast the performance.
Geography	*Breadth of study* Any of themes a to e	Select a geographical item currently in the local or national news. Research the story and use the information as the basis for creating a magazine article or newspaper report. (Link to *Making a Splash, Micro Man Makes Big News* and *The Big Story*)
Art and design/ICT	*Breadth of study* a) exploring a range of starting points c) using a range of processes including ICT	Explore how different fonts, layout, print size, illustrations and other graphic devices are used to create an eye catching page in newspapers and magazines. Create an on screen newspaper page using these. (Link to *Making a Splash, Micro Man Makes Big News* and *WOW!*)
History	*11b) Britain since 1930* Study of social and technological changes	Research how the reporting of news has changed over the last century - from silent newsreels to instant satellite and internet broadcasting. Or look at how newspapers and news magazines have changed, particularly the layout and use of language and images. (Link to *Making a Splash, Micro Man Makes Big News* and *The Big Story*)
Music/ ICT	*Music breadth of study* a) musical activities that involve ... composing and performing b) responding to a range of starting points *ICT breadth of study* b) Working with others to explore a variety of information sources and ICT tools	Listen to and analyse the theme music for TV news bulletins. Compose theme music for a news programme. Create, film, record, edit and broadcast a news report relating to the news item being studied in geography or science. Use the music composed for the opening sequence of the broadcast. (Link to *Making a Splash, Micro Man Makes Big News* and *The Big Story*)
PSHE/citizenship	*2 Preparing to play an active role as a citizen* k) explore how the media present information	Look at how an event is depicted in books, TV, radio, newspapers, and on the internet. Compare and contrast similarities and differences. (Link to *Making a Splash*) You could use the above exercise to look at how celebrities are presented in the media and hold a discussion about the pros and cons of being famous. (Link to *The WOW! Award*)

Name ....

Story flow diagram

Teacher instruction: You may need to provide children with more than one copy of this Photocopy Master.

Record your route through the story by noting the key events in the boxes provided. When there is a **?** > or **O**, add this to the circle at the bottom of each box. The first one has been done for you.

Page 2-5 The children discover that the statue is missing. They split up to investigate. **(?)**	**Page** _____	**Page** _____
Page _____	**Page** _____	**Page** _____
Page _____	**Page** _____	**Page** _____
Page _____	**Page** _____	**Page** _____

Talking frame

Making a Stand – Chapter 1

Retell Chapter 1 from Dani's point of view. Use the pictures to help you.

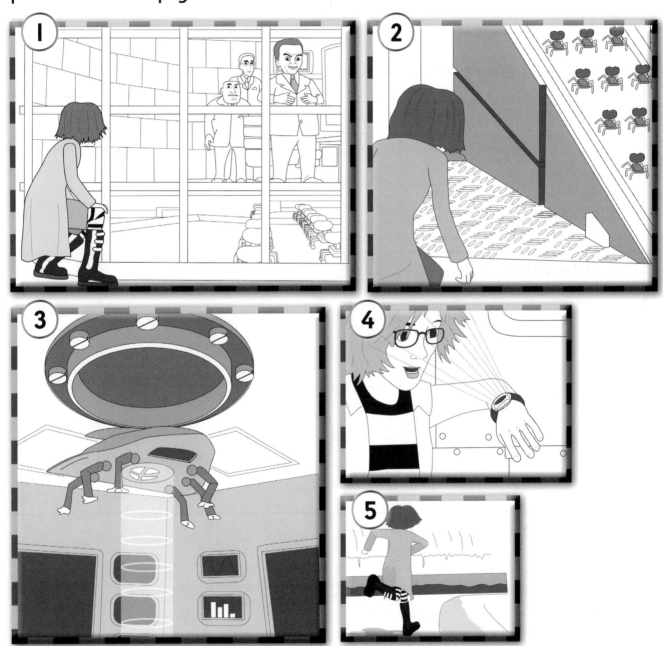

Questions for the listening partner

Did your partner include all the important actions?

Did your partner use expression in their voice?

Did your partner use interesting words?

Name ....

It's Your Call summary

3

Title of section
The problem is   Evidence of this problem   •   •   •
Possible solutions
I think I could help by

Name ....

It's Your Call writing frame

It's Your Call

One of the things that contributes to environmental problems is

_____

_____

_____

It causes

_____

_____

People help to create this problem by

_____

_____

They could help improve this problem by

_____

_____

I think

_____

_____

_____

Name ....

What are they saying?

Name ....

Nicknames

Proper Name	Friendly nickname	Why called this?	Cruel nickname	Why called this?
Edward Quick				
Sean Hawkes				
Mr Rose				
	Big Harry			

Project X: Grey band – Dilemmas and Decisions – The Witness

Name ....

Relationship grid

Make notes on this grid to show how the characters interact with each other.

	Max	Cat	Tiger	Ant
Max				
Cat				
Tiger				
Ant				

Name ....

Using the writer's craft

> *With a great roaring of engines, the X-craft finally docked inside the giant sphere at the top of the NICE building. The doors slid closed around them.*

You will notice that the writer has begun with a complex sentence and then used a short compound sentence to finish the paragraph. Use this sentence model to create your own opening paragraph:

With a _____

_____

The _____

Now look at some of the other sentences on page 4. Collect some of the sentences that you would like to copy and use them as a model to create your own sentences.

_____
_____
_____
_____
_____
_____
_____

Name ....

Newspaper report

Title of newspaper

Headline

Article

Picture

Name ....

Olaudah's account

Reread Olaudah's account of how he was captured by slave traders. Write any unusual words and phrases he has used. In a different colour highlight the phrases that have an unusual word order. Now try to write the next sentence that he might have written using the same style that he has used.

Unusual words and phrases	Next sentence could be...

Project X: Grey band – Great Escapes – Escaping Slavery

Name ....

Relationship grid

As you read through the story, make notes on this grid about how the characters interact with each other.

	Calvin	George	Mei Ling	Gabriella	Berko
Calvin					
George					
Mei Ling					
Gabriella					
Berko					

Name ....

Character profiles

Choose one of the main characters from the story.
Draw a portrait and write a short description for the
character you choose.

Profile

Portrait

Name_____

_____

_____

Appearance _____

_____

_____

_____

_____

Characteristics_____

_____

_____

_____

_____

_____

Name ....

Escapes from Colditz

List the main features and decide the good and bad things about each escape.

Section	Main features of the escape	Good/Bad Points
MI9 – Escape school		
Making a good impression		
Masters of disguise		
Going underground		
Over and out		
Up and away		

Dr X and Mrs X said ...

Write what Dr X and his mum might have said to each other when they were in jail.

Name ....

Comic strip writing frame

Create a comic strip of the day's main events in
The WOW! Award

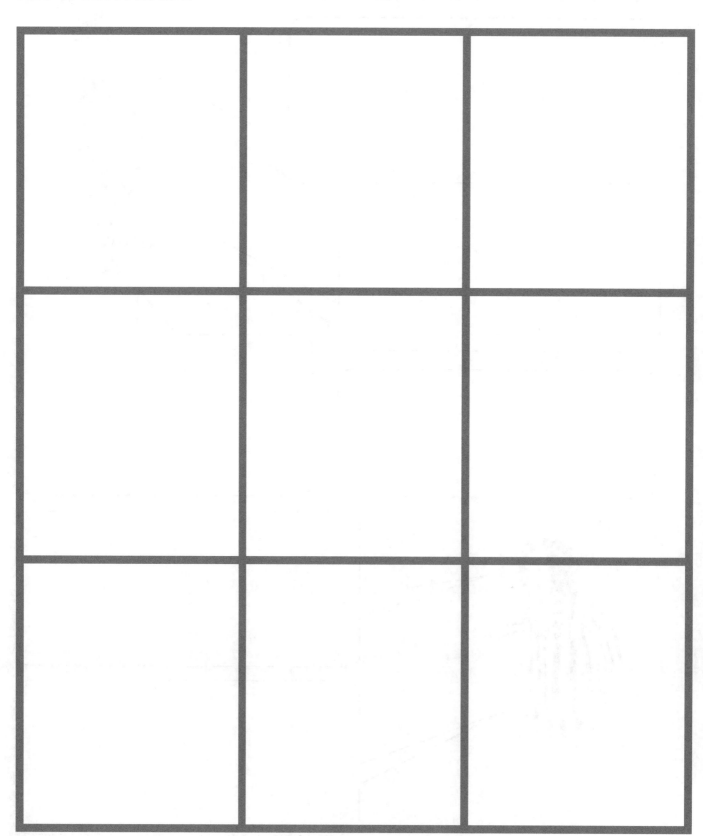

Project X: Grey band – In the News – The WOW! Award

Name ....

Book review

Write a book review using the headings below.

Picture:

Title:

Author:

Plot:

| Excitement: /10 | Fear Factor: /10 | Easy Read: /10 | Humour: /10 |

Name ....

Our favourite books

Use this graph to find out what your favourite class book is. Each child can draw one star beside their favourite book.

20				
19				
18				
17				
16				
15				
14				
13				
12				
11				
10				
9				
8				
7				
6				
5				
4				
3				
2				
1				
	Name of book	Name of book	Name of book	Name of book

Project X: Grey band – In the News – WOW!

Name ....

What do we know about Willard?

Collect information about Willard Wigan as you read *Micro Man Makes Big News*. Write direct quotes and information in the speech bubbles. Put information that you have inferred in the thought bubbles.

Project X: Grey band – In the News – Micro Man Makes Big News

Name ....

Direct and reported speech

Look through *Micro Man Makes Big News* and note down examples of the different types of speech.

Direct speech	Reported speech

Name ....

UltraGym

Design a poster to advertise UltraGym. Remember you will need to use exaggeration to persuade people! Think about other persuasive techniques you could use.

Project X: Grey band – In the News – The Big Story

Name ....

Subject and journalistic words

Find new words in *Making a Splash* and write their meanings.

Whale words

Word	Definition

News report words

Word	Definition

Name ....

Character profile

Draw a picture of a character from a story or invent your
own character. Make notes about them.

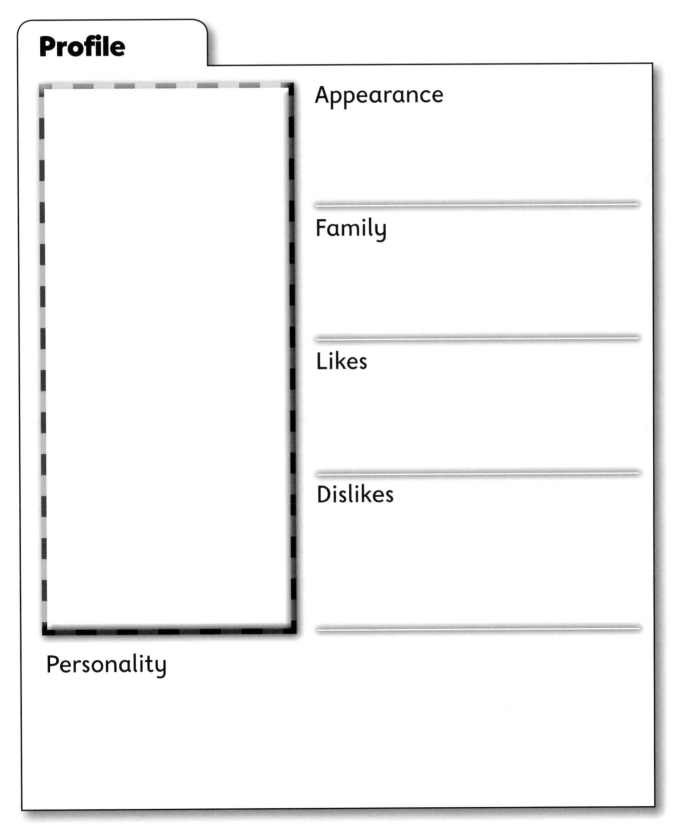

Profile

Appearance

Family

Likes

Dislikes

Personality

Name ....

Character log

Make notes about a character from a story, or invent your own character.

I am ...
I live ...
I have ...
I like ...
I don't like ...
Anything else?

Name ....

Character relationships grid

Use this grid to record the relationships between different characters in a story. Write in the names of the characters. Make notes in each box to show character relationships (e.g. mother/son) and what the characters think of each other.

Book title: _____

Author: _____

	Character 1	Character 2	Character 3	Character 4
Character 1				
Character 2				
Character 3				
Character 4				

Name ....

Prediction and reflection grid

What do you think might happen in the book? Make notes in the first two columns before you read the book.

What did happen in the book? Make notes in the last column after reading.

Book title Author		
I think this might happen …	I think this because …	What did happen

Name ....

Episode analysis

Use this grid to help you think carefully about important points in a story.

Book title **Author**		
Outline the key event	What does this tell you about the character/s?	What do you think of their actions?
	Why is this event important in the story?	

Name ....

Inference grid

After reading a book, think about what you know and what you learned.

Book title
Author

What I know about from reading the book

What I know about from clues in the book and my own thinking
(Think about what you can work out from the words not just what the words say)

Name ....

Synthesizing grid (1 + 1 = 2)

Use this chart to help you make links between the information in different parts of a book. What new information do you find by adding up the facts?

Book title Author		
I found this out on page …	I found this out on page …	These two things together tell me …
I found this out on page …	I found this out on page …	These two things together tell me …
I found this out on page …	I found this out on page …	These two things together tell me …

Name ....

Think, feel, say ...

Make notes about a character in a book. What does the character think, feel and say?

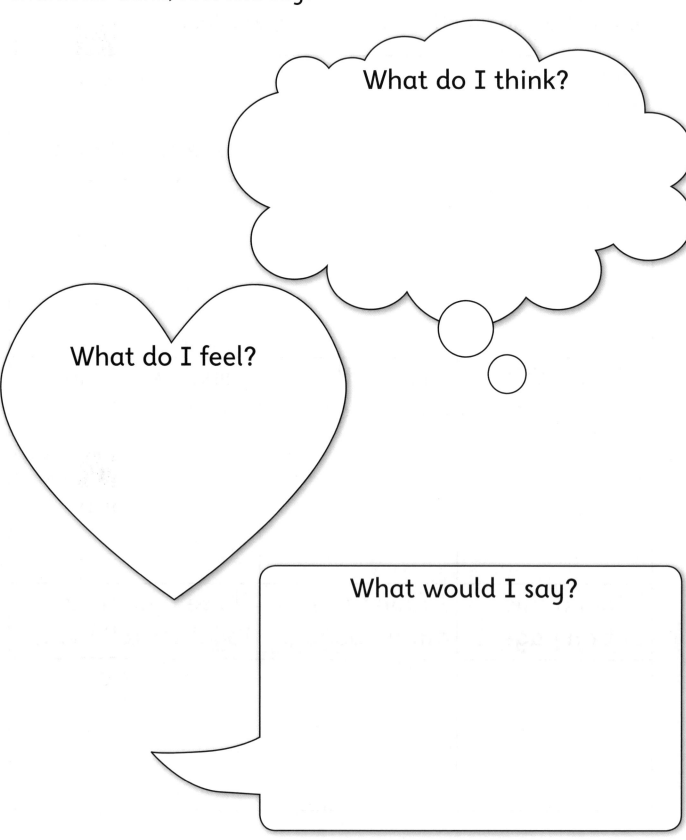

What do I think?

What do I feel?

What would I say?

Name ....

Cause and effect

Use these tables to record events and their effects.

Fiction

CAUSE	EFFECT
What did the character do?	What happened because of this?
What is the event?	What happened as a result?

Non-fiction

CAUSE	EFFECT
What is the event?	What happened as a result?
What is the step in the process?	What happens as a result?

Name ....

Compare and contrast information

Use this grid to compare and contrast information from different non-fiction sources – e.g. books, magazines, video clips, the internet.

Information source 1	Information source 2	Information source 3
Title:	Title:	Title:
What I found out …	What I found out …	What I found out …

Name ....

Before and after reading

Use this grid to compare what you know before reading a book with what you know after reading.

Statement	Before reading			After reading		
	True ✓	False ✗	Don't know ?	True ✓	False ✗	Don't know ?

Name ....

Vocabulary detective

Use this sheet to record new words you meet when reading.
List the word and its meaning.

Book title Author	
New word	**Word meaning**

Name ....

Author words

Authors choose words and phrases carefully. In stories, they choose words to create mood or to create a 'picture' of a setting or character. In information books, they choose words to explain a topic or theme.

As you read a book, use this chart to record the interesting words and phrases that the author uses.

Book title: _____

Author: _____

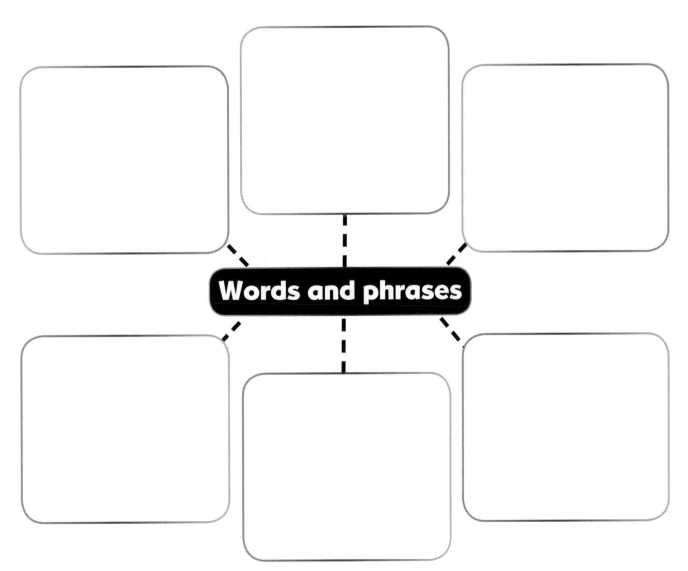

Name ....

Note taking

Use this grid to help you make notes from your reading.
Don't forget to add the page numbers in case you need
to check your notes.

Book 1 Title:					
	Main fact				
	Details				

Book 2 Title:					
	Main fact				
	Details				